SADLIER'S
New Catholic School
Coming to Faith Program

COMING TO
THE CHURCH

Dr. Gerard F. Baumbach

Dr. Eleanor Ann Brownell

Moya Gullage

Joan B. Collins

Helen Hemmer, I. H. M.

Gloria Hutchinson

Dr. Norman F. Josaitis

Rev. Michael J. Lanning, O. F. M.

Dr. Marie Murphy

Karen Ryan

Joseph F. Sweeney

Patricia Andrews

with

Dr. Thomas H. Groome
Boston College

Official Theological Consultant
  Rev. Edward K. Braxton, Ph. D., S. T. D.

Scriptural Consultant
  Rev. Donald Senior, C. P., Ph. D., S. T. D.

Catechetical and Liturgical Consultants
  Dr. Gerard F. Baumbach
  Dr. Eleanor Ann Brownell

Pastoral Consultants
  Rev. Msgr. John F. Barry
  Rev. Virgilio P. Elizondo, Ph. D., S. T. D.

Catechetical Assessment Consultant
  Dr. George Elford

William H. Sadlier, Inc.
9 Pine Street
New York, New York 10005-1002

Nihil Obstat
✠ Most Reverend George O. Wirz
Censor Librorum

Imprimatur
✠ Most Reverend William H. Bullock
Bishop of Madison
December 30, 1994

The *Nihil Obstat* and *Imprimatur* are official declarations that a book or pamphlet is free of doctrinal or moral error. No implication is contained therein that those who have granted the *Nihil Obstat* and *Imprimatur* agree with the contents, opinions, or statements expressed.

Printed in the United States of America.

Credits appear on page 288.

Home Office:
9 Pine Street
New York, NY 10005–1002

ISBN: 0-8215-3303-7
3456789/9876

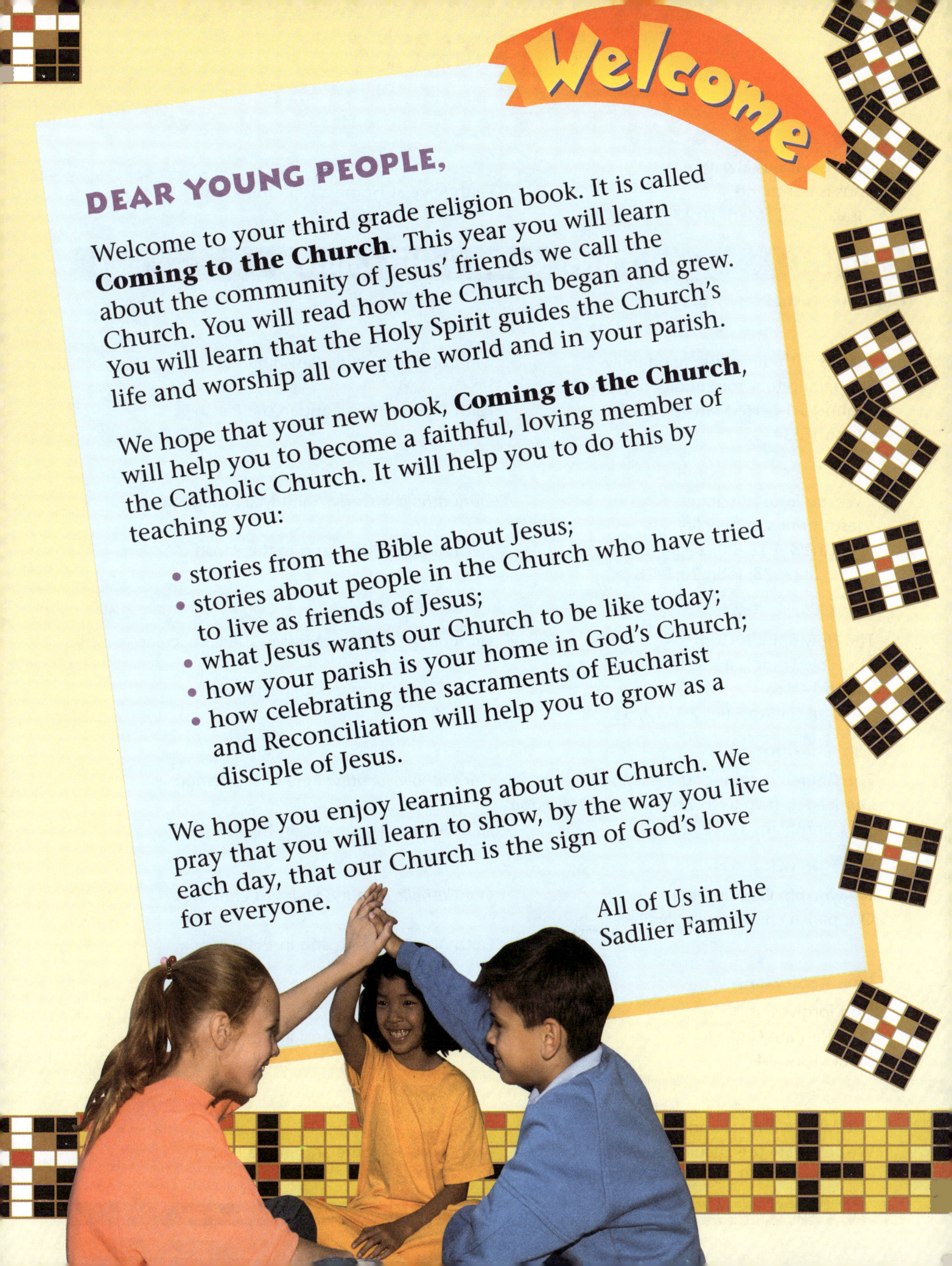

Welcome

DEAR YOUNG PEOPLE,

Welcome to your third grade religion book. It is called **Coming to the Church**. This year you will learn about the community of Jesus' friends we call the Church. You will read how the Church began and grew. You will learn that the Holy Spirit guides the Church's life and worship all over the world and in your parish.

We hope that your new book, **Coming to the Church**, will help you to become a faithful, loving member of the Catholic Church. It will help you to do this by teaching you:

- stories from the Bible about Jesus;
- stories about people in the Church who have tried to live as friends of Jesus;
- what Jesus wants our Church to be like today;
- how your parish is your home in God's Church;
- how celebrating the sacraments of Eucharist and Reconciliation will help you to grow as a disciple of Jesus.

We hope you enjoy learning about our Church. We pray that you will learn to show, by the way you live each day, that our Church is the sign of God's love for everyone.

All of Us in the
Sadlier Family

CONTENTS

Jesus is with us always
Jesus is our friend   Faith Alive at Home and in the Parish
   Isaiah 43:1; Mark 10:13–16

Unit 1	Jesus Christ Gives Us His Church	page

Doctrine: Catholic Teaching

Jesus is with our parish and family   *Our Catholic Identity:* Parish names
We belong to a community of Jesus' friends
   John 15:14–16; Matthew 28:19;   Faith Alive at Home and in the Parish
   John 13:34–35

We are Jesus' disciples   *Our Catholic Identity:* Saint Mary Magdalene
Jesus brings us new life
   Matthew 4:18–20; 22:34–39;   Faith Alive at Home and in the Parish
   Luke 5:27–28; John 20:1–18

The Holy Spirit is God   *Our Catholic Identity:* Mass in the vernacular
The Holy Spirit is a special helper
   John 14:16;   Faith Alive at Home and in the Parish
   Acts of the Apostles 2:1–12, 33, 38

The Church continues the mission of Jesus   *Our Catholic Identity:* Role of the bishop
Our leaders help us to work for God's kingdom
   1 Corinthians 12:12–27   Faith Alive at Home and in the Parish

We worship God together   *Our Catholic Identity:* Styles of churches
Our parish church is a holy place
          Faith Alive at Home and in the Parish

God forgives us
We celebrate God's love   Faith Alive at Home and in the Parish
   John 15:9–14

The Mass is a meal and a sacrifice
We celebrate the Eucharist   Faith Alive at Home and in the Parish
   Matthew 28:20

Unit 1 Review and Unit 1 Test—see Pages 261–262

OPENING PRAYER SERVICE

Call to Prayer (All): In the name of the Father, and of the Son, and of the Holy Spirit. Amen.

Teacher: This year we will discover more about being followers of Jesus in the Catholic Church. Let us look at the front cover of our religion book. What do you see in the mosaic? Why do you think there are so many flowers in the picture?

First Child: We know that flowers come from seeds and seeds need certain things to grow.

Teacher: Can you name some things seeds need to grow?

Second Child: Our faith, like seeds, also needs certain things to grow.

Teacher: Who are some of the people who will help us grow in our faith?

Have you ever planted seeds? Today we are going to plant some seeds in our bowl of soil, our faith garden. As these seeds grow and become strong and beautiful plants, they will remind us that we are growing as followers of Jesus and that we can help others grow, too.

Third Child: Scripture Reading
Jesus told a story about a farmer who planted seeds. Jesus said, "Some seed fell on good soil. The plants from this seed grew healthy and large and gave a lot of grain."
From Matthew 13:8

Fourth Child: Closing Prayer
Let us join hands as we ask God to help us grow in faith. Let us pray the prayer Jesus taught us: "Our Father. . . ."

Our New Year Begins!

Dear Jesus,
teach us how to
follow You.

Our Life

On life's exciting journey,
God says to each one of us,
"I have called you by your name—
you are Mine."
From Isaiah 43:1

Just think! God knows your name!
God knows you and loves you.

By what special name does God
know you?

Make sure everyone in the group
knows your name.

Sharing Life

Make a name plate for yourself and
decorate it with your favorite
designs and colors.

On the back finish each sentence.
I love . . .
I wish . . .
I can . . .
Share what you have written with
one another. Then put all your
nameplates together and make
a poster or banner.

What does it mean for you that
God knows your name?

Share your feelings together.

9

JESUS

Jesus Our Friend

This is a Bible story that shows Jesus' great love for all children. Some parents brought their children to Jesus. But Jesus was very tired. His friends wanted to send the children away. "No," Jesus said. "Let the children come to Me and do not stop them, because the kingdom of God belongs to them."

Then Jesus took the children in His arms, placed His hands on each of them, and blessed them.
From Mark 10:13–16

What a good friend Jesus is to children! Put yourself in the picture to show you want to be a friend of Jesus, too.

This year we will learn more about Jesus, our true friend. We will learn how we can be His followers, or disciples, in the Catholic Church.

JESUS

Is there something you would like to know about Jesus? Is there something special you would like to ask Him or tell Him?

Write a letter to Jesus. Tell or ask Him anything you wish. We will keep all our letters in a special place. We will look at them again at the end of the year.

Perhaps some of our thoughts and questions will have been answered. Perhaps we will find we have more questions to ask Jesus.

11

Coming To Faith

Act out the gospel story of Jesus and the children with your friends.

How does this story make you feel about Jesus?

Practicing Faith

Our religion group will be like a little "Church" this year. We will pray and learn and work together as followers, or disciples, of Jesus, our true friend.

Let's gather in a friendship circle and pray in words or in song our closing prayer. (To the tune of "Amazing Grace")

♫ O Jesus, You're our friend indeed,
You're with us every day.
Oh help us all to follow You
In all we do and say.

Help us to learn about the Church
And how to love like You.
We want to be Your best of friends
In all we say and do. ♫

Show the children the "Faith Alive" section. Remind them to go over the *Faith Summary* with their parents.

12

REVIEW

Unscramble the letters written in each picture. What will we do together this year?

We will  (yarp) and  (rnela)

and  (rowk) together as  (psidciels) of Jesus.

We will be like a "  (ltltie) Church."

FAITH ALIVE AT HOME AND IN THE PARISH

This year your third grader will learn more about following Jesus as a member of the Catholic Church. As you help your child experience community, first in your family and then in your parish, you are preparing your daughter or son for full participation in the life of the Church. It is important to nourish this growth by bringing your child to Mass each Saturday evening or Sunday. Talk with your child about the Faith Summary statements that summarize each chapter.

 Learn by heart **Faith Summary**

- Jesus welcomed and blessed the children.

- Jesus is with us always. He is our friend.

1 Parish, Family, and Me

Dear God,
thank You for
my family.

OUR LIFE

Lia had been an orphan for most of her eight years. Then one day she was told that a family wanted to adopt her. Lia was excited and a little afraid. But her new family was wonderful. It was big, warm, loving, and noisy.

Lia was very happy, but she had one question. One night at supper she asked, "Why did you adopt me? Wouldn't you rather have had your own baby?"

Everybody started talking at once! "No, no. We wanted you," Mom said. "You belong to us," Dad said. "You're fun!" yelled the twins. "I always wanted a little sister," said Angie.

Lia smiled. She liked being in this family. She felt really at home.

Tell about your family. Share what you like most about it.

SHARING LIFE

How does Jesus want us to live as members of our own family? of our parish family?

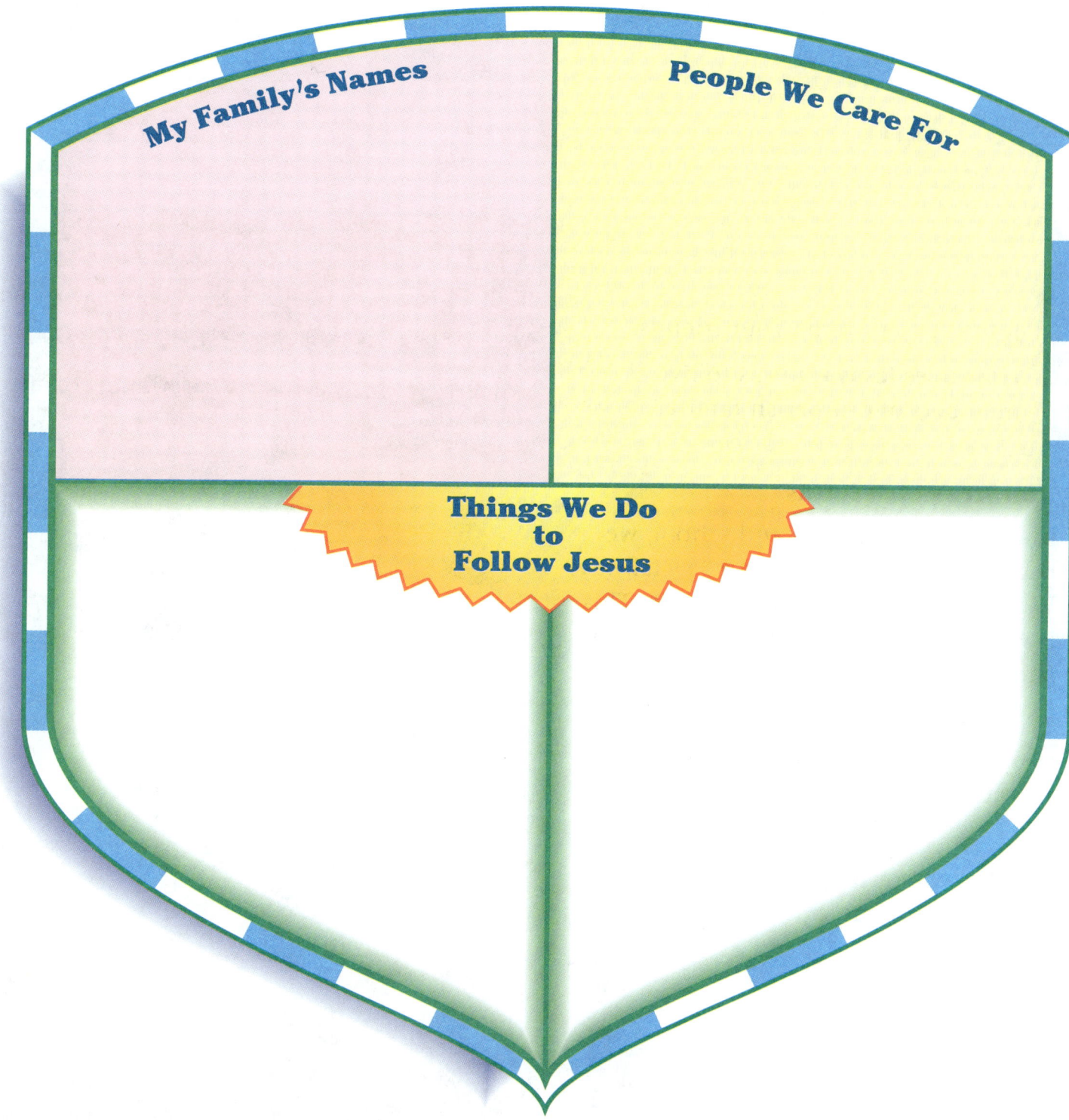

My Family's Names

People We Care For

Things We Do
to
Follow Jesus

Decorate the shield to show how your family tries to live as Jesus wants us to live. Share your shield with your friends.

Talk about something you can do as a class to show that you are friends of Jesus.

In this lesson we will discover how Jesus helps us to live together as a community of His friends.

We Will Learn

- Jesus is our friend.
- Jesus is with us in our families.
- Jesus wants us to be a community.

OUR CATHOLIC FAITH

- Jesus, help us to be Your friends.
- How does Jesus want us to live as members of our parish family?

You Are My Friends

In our Catholic parish and school, we learn that Jesus loves us in a special way. We learn to live as friends of Jesus. This is what Jesus says to us about being His friends:

"You are My friends if you do as I command you. I do not call you servants. I call you friends. I chose you."
From John 15:14–16

What a wonderful gift it is to be friends with Jesus!

A **parish** is a group of Jesus' disciples who worship God together.

Jesus wants to be a good friend to everyone. Jesus said to His first followers:

"Go to all people everywhere and make them My disciples. Baptize them in the name of the Father, the Son, and the Holy Spirit."
From Matthew 28:19

To be a disciple means to be a friend of Jesus, to follow His example. Through Baptism, we first became friends of Jesus. In our parish family, we learn that Jesus Christ is with us. He helps us to live as His friends.

By the way we treat one another, it should be easy for people to see that Jesus is with us and that we are His friends, His disciples.

Write what you will do to show you are a friend of Jesus.

_____

_____

_____

_____

- What does Jesus tell us about being His friends?

- How will you show that you are a friend of Jesus?

17

OUR CATHOLIC FAITH

- Listen to and then sing "O Jesus, You're our friend indeed." (See page 12.)

- Tell about some happy things you do with your family.

Jesus in Our Family

Like all of us, Jesus had a family. He lived with His mother, Mary, and His foster father, Joseph, in a small town named Nazareth.

Jesus, Mary, and Joseph worked, played, and prayed together. We call Jesus, Mary, and Joseph the Holy Family.

Jesus is with us in our families. Not all families are alike. Some have two parents and some have one. Some families are large and others are small. But no matter what kind of family we belong to, Jesus is with us. He shows us how to love one another.

We live as Jesus wants us to live when we care for one another in our families. We can help our families to grow as friends of Jesus.

We can also learn to pray in our families. We can pray with our families in the morning and at night. We can pray before and after meals.

Jesus is with us in our **families** when we are happy and when we are sad. Some families are not always happy. This may be hard for us to understand.

When our families are happy, we should thank Jesus. When our families are sad, we can talk to Jesus about it. Jesus is always there to help us. He understands the fears and worries that all of us have and that are a part of life.

Jesus does not want us to hold our hurts inside. We should ask our **parents**, our teacher, our priest, or some other adult to help us.

Write how you will try to help your family today.

_____

_____

_____

_____

▪ Can you share something with your family about Jesus?

▪ Dear God, please help our families to be more like the Holy Family.

19

OUR CATHOLIC FAITH

■ God of love, please bless my family.

■ What do you like best about being a friend of Jesus?

Jesus in Our Community

Jesus taught us how to be His friends. He gathered people together and showed them how to do God's will. Jesus taught people to believe and to trust in God. But most important of all, He taught people to love. Jesus said:

"As I have loved you, so you must love one another. Everyone will know that you are My friends if you love one another."
From John 13:34–35

By our love for one another, we show that we are Jesus' community. We gather in our parish church to pray together and to learn to love all people. We trust Jesus to love us and to hear our prayers.

By the loving things we do for other people, we tell everyone that we belong to the community of Jesus' friends, the Church.

Learning About Your Parish Name

Every Catholic in the world belongs to a parish. Each parish has its own name. The name of a parish comes from one of our beliefs about God, Mary, or the saints.

Perhaps you belong to a parish named Christ the King or Our Lady of Guadalupe or Saint Sebastian.

Have you ever tried to find out about the name of your parish? What you discover may surprise you. For example, there is a parish called Curé of Ars. It is named after Saint John Vianney. He was a parish priest in a small village in France called Ars. He was a very holy man. He is the patron saint of parish priests.

Discover more about the name of your parish. Then share your findings with your class.

Learn by heart **Faith Summary**

- Jesus is our friend.
- Jesus is with us in our family and in our parish.
- Jesus wants us to be a community of His disciples.

21

Coming To Faith

How is your family a community of Jesus' friends?

How is your parish a community of Jesus' disciples?

Show the world that Jesus is your friend. Decorate this banner.

Are you happy to be Jesus' friend? Why?

Practicing Faith

Sit in a friendship circle. Talk together about ways you will be disciples of Jesus in your families.

Then think about ways you will be disciples of Jesus in your parish. Is there something you can do together as a group? Share your ideas. Join hands and pray the Our Father together.

Talk with your teacher about ways you and your family can use the "Faith Alive" section. You might especially want to share how you will try to make your family happy.

22

REVIEW ∙ TEST

Circle the letter beside the correct answer.

1. To be a disciple of Jesus means to love
   a. only our friends.
   b. as Jesus loved.
   c. little children.

2. Jesus told His followers to baptize
   a. some people.
   b. all people.
   c. only their friends.

3. We show we are Jesus' community by
   a. doing loving things for others.
   b. making our friends happy.
   c. being selfish.

4. The most important thing Jesus taught us is to
   a. believe.
   b. trust.
   c. love.

5. Write how you can be a friend of Jesus.

_____

FAITH ALIVE — AT HOME AND IN THE PARISH

In this lesson your child learned that Jesus taught us how to be His friends. Talk with your child about ways we show that we are friends of Jesus at home, at school, and in our parish. Stress that when we do loving things for one another, we tell everyone that we belong to Jesus' community of friends. Highlight the fact that Catholic parishes are communities of worship centered on the Eucharist. Nourished by God's word in Scripture and by the Body and Blood of Christ, we serve the spiritual and human needs of all.

Christian Helpers

Have your family find and cut out magazine or newspaper pictures of people who help others. Paste the pictures on a large piece of paper.

Between the pictures write the names of people you know who help others. At the top of the paper write "Pictures of Things Christians Should Do." Bring your poster to school to share with your classmates.

Secret Promises

Give each family member a slip of paper labeled "My Secret Promise." On the reverse have each person write one thing he or she will try to do this week to be a more caring family member. At the end of the week share the secret promises and one another's experiences of trying to keep them. Together, ask Jesus to help you continue to grow as a loving family.

23

2 Jesus Calls His Followers

Jesus, help us
to follow You.

Our Life

One day, Jesus was walking beside
the Sea of Galilee. He saw two
brothers fishing. Their names were
Simon and Andrew. Jesus waited for
them to come back to shore and then
said to them, "Come, follow Me."

At once, Simon and Andrew dropped
their nets and followed Jesus.
From Matthew 4:18–20

Jesus was now their leader. Simon
and Andrew became followers, or
disciples, of Jesus.

Tell what a good leader is like.
Tell about times when you were a
good leader. Tell about times when
you were a good follower.

Sharing Life

How do you think Jesus wanted Simon
and Andrew to follow Him?

What are some things Jesus wants to
teach all His disciples? Make a
list together.

Now fill out your own "Disciple of Jesus" membership card.

Come, Follow Jesus

Name: _____

Disciple since: _____

Some things Jesus wants to teach me:

_____

_____

_____

_____

This year, I will try to learn more about what it means to be a disciple of Jesus.

Disciple of Jesus

Signature _____

Share your card with a friend.

In this lesson we will discover that Jesus calls His disciples to bring the good news of God's love to others.

We Will Learn

- Jesus invited people to be His disciples.

- Jesus taught His disciples to live the Law of Love.

- Jesus died and rose from the dead.

■ Jesus, teach us how to be Your followers.

■ How do you like being a follower of Jesus?

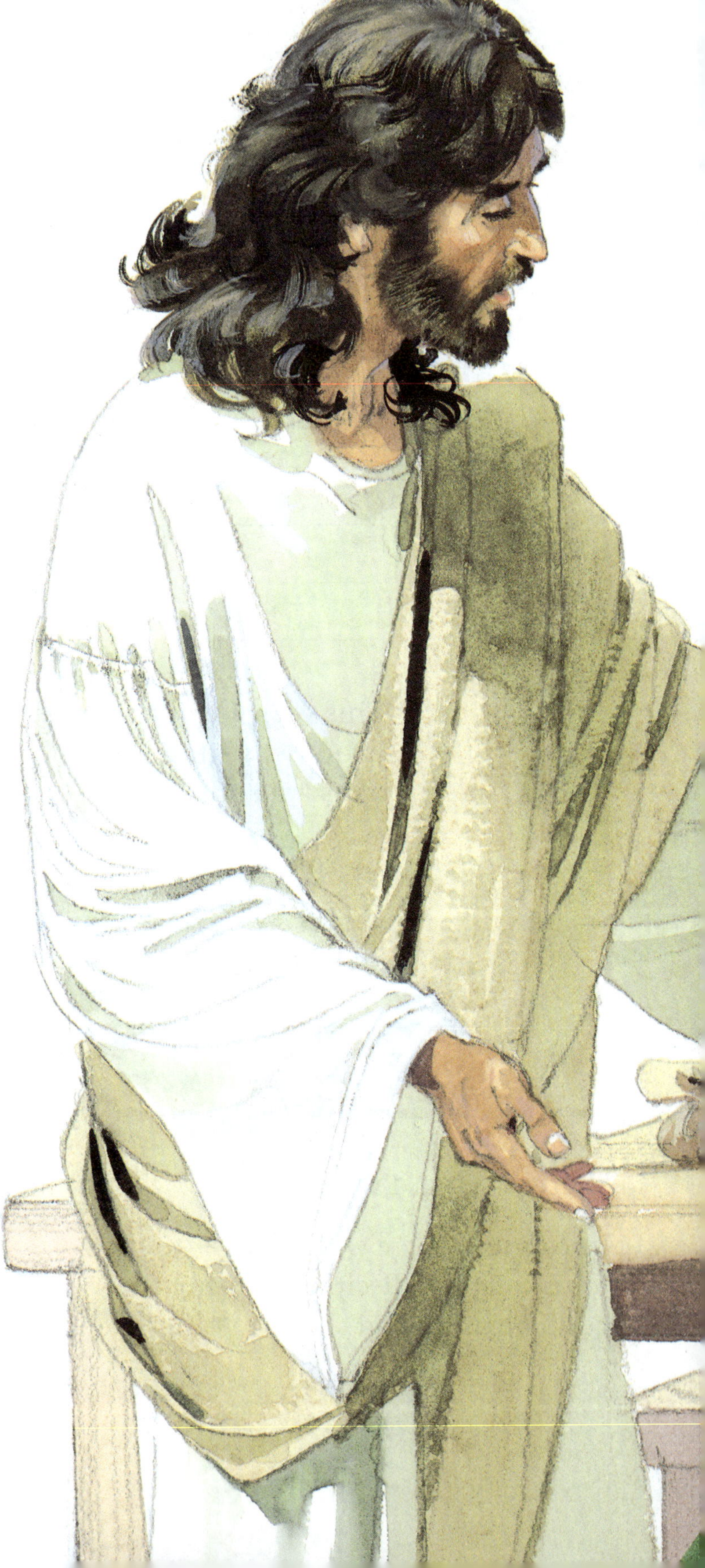

Jesus Invited His Disciples

When Jesus grew up, He knew that He had something special to do for God. He was to tell and show all people the good news of God's kingdom. Jesus showed people how much God loved them. He also showed them how to do God's will.

Jesus knew that He would need helpers for this great mission. He began to gather His community of followers. We call Jesus' followers His disciples.

One day, Jesus saw a tax collector named Matthew sitting at his collection table. Most people hated the tax collectors. But Jesus said to Matthew, "Come, follow Me." He left everything and followed Jesus.

From Luke 5:27–28

Jesus' mission was His work of bringing the good news of God's love to the world.

Jesus' community of disciples started to grow. Soon, large crowds followed Jesus. People came to hear and see Him. Many of them left everything to follow Him.

Jesus later chose some of these closest followers to lead the other disciples. We call these first leaders the apostles.

Jesus invites us to be His disciples, too. Jesus Christ is our greatest leader. He wants us to be His followers. He shows us how to live as God's people.

■ What did Jesus show His disciples?

■ Name one thing you will do today because you are a disciple of Jesus.

OUR CATHOLIC FAITH

- Jesus, thank You for calling us to be Your disciples.

- Make a list of things that Jesus' disciples do.

Jesus Taught His Disciples

When Jesus began to tell the good news, crowds of people came. They wanted to hear what He said and to see what He did. Jesus taught the people how to love God, one another, and themselves.

One day a teacher of the law came to Jesus. He wanted to trap Jesus. The man asked a question that he thought would get Jesus into trouble. He asked, "Which commandment is the most important of all?"

Jesus answered, "Love God with all your heart and love your neighbor as yourself." From Matthew 22:34–39

This was the greatest lesson that Jesus taught His followers. We call it the Law of Love.

Jesus also taught His disciples how to pray. One day, one of His disciples said to Him, "Lord, teach us to pray." Jesus taught them a very special prayer.

We still say the prayer that Jesus taught His disciples. We call it the Our Father.

Jesus said He came to give all people His peace. Peace can mean many things. Peace means not having war. Peace means not fighting. Peace means respecting everyone. We cannot have Jesus' peace without justice. Justice means making sure that everyone is treated fairly.

We are Jesus' disciples. We are to love God, others, and ourselves. We are to pray. We are to treat everyone fairly and to be peacemakers, too.

Find four important words from the Law of Love on page 28. Print them in the puzzle.

■ How will you try to be a peacemaker today?

■ Pray the Our Father with your group.

29

OUR CATHOLIC FAITH

■ Jesus, help us to live the Law of Love.

■ Imagine yourself really living the Law of Love. Share your imaginings with your friends.

Jesus Died and Rose

Not everyone wanted to live the way of Jesus. Some people were jealous of Jesus and wanted to put Him to death. Jesus was arrested, tortured, and put to death on the cross. Jesus gave His life for us to save us from sin. We call the day Jesus died Good Friday.

Early on the next Sunday morning, Mary Magdalene, a friend of Jesus, went to the tomb where Jesus was buried. The tomb was empty. Mary saw someone standing nearby. It was Jesus. Jesus was alive! He had risen from the dead. Jesus told Mary to go and tell all His disciples.
From John 20:1–18

We call the day Jesus rose from the dead Easter Sunday.

Jesus rose from the dead to bring us new life. Because of the risen Christ, we can live forever with God.

The risen Jesus is with us today. He calls us to live this new life as His disciples.

Saint Mary Magdalene

Saint Mary Magdalene was a loyal friend of Jesus. When Jesus was dying on the cross, Mary Magdalene was there with the mother of Jesus to comfort Him. After Jesus died, she went to the tomb to anoint His body.

Mary Magdalene was one of the first people to receive the news that Jesus had risen. She was the first person to see the risen Jesus. She was the one whom Jesus sent to tell the other disciples that He was alive. For this reason, the Church often calls Mary Magdalene the "apostle of the apostles."

Read again the story of Mary Magdalene on page 30. Imagine her joy and wonder when she recognized her friend the risen Jesus.

Ask Saint Mary Magdalene to pray for you, so that you may recognize the risen Jesus in your life, too. We celebrate the feast of Saint Mary Magdalene on July 22.

Learn by heart **Faith Summary**

- Jesus' followers are called disciples.
- Jesus invites us to be His disciples.
- Jesus died and rose from the dead to bring us new life.

COMING TO FAITH

Form a circle with two of your friends in the middle. They will be Simon and Andrew. Then sing to the tune of "Yankee Doodle":

♪ Simon, who came up to you
That day when you were fishing?
What did the stranger say to you?
And oh, what did you answer?
   ("Simon" answers.)

Andrew, tell us how you felt
When you heard Jesus call you.
And tell us why you followed Him
To be His true disciple. ♪
   ("Andrew" answers.)

Now imagine Jesus saying to you, "Come, follow Me." How would you answer?

PRACTICING FAITH

Sit in your circle. Talk with one another about ways the members of your group will live as disciples of Jesus this week.

Choose one thing you will do this week in your parish to show that you are learning to be a disciple of Jesus.

Talk with your teacher about ways you and your family might use the "Faith Alive" section. Pray the Family Prayer with your family.

REVIEW ■ TEST

Circle the letter beside the correct answer.

1. The first leaders Jesus chose were called

   a. tax collectors.   **b.** apostles.   **c.** fishermen.

2. Jesus died on

   a. Good Friday.   **b.** Easter Sunday.   **c.** Holy Thursday.

3. The prayer Jesus taught us is the

   a. Sign of the Cross. **b.** Our Father.   **c.** Hail Mary.

4. Jesus rose from the dead to bring us

   a. new life.   **b.** miracles.   **c.** the Bible.

5. How will you be a peacemaker this week?

_____

_____

FAITH ALIVE — AT HOME AND IN THE PARISH

In this lesson your child learned that Jesus invites each of us to be His disciple. Your child also learned more about our call as disciples to live the Law of Love. As we enter more fully into the celebration of Christ's saving death and resurrection (the paschal mystery), we are enabled to live the new life Christ shares with us. For example, all of us experience times of difficulty in our lives. But we can live with the confidence that the Holy Spirit strengthens us to meet life's challenges. Talk with your child about the importance of showing love for God, others, and ourselves by praying, by treating everyone fairly, and by being peacemakers. Remember, too, how important it is for you to help your child truly to love himself or herself.

Love Box

On a small box write these words: "Disciples of Jesus love one another." Have the members of your family write their names on separate slips of paper. If you wish, include the names of friends, relatives, and parish members. Fold the slips of paper and put them in the box. Then ask each family member to pick a name and agree to do something loving for that person. Depending on the number of names in the box, you may want to continue this activity over several weeks.

† Family Prayer

Join hands and pray the special prayer Jesus taught His disciples: "Our Father, who art in heaven. . . ."

3 The Church Begins

Holy Spirit, fill us with courage to live our faith.

OUR LIFE

Disciples of Jesus sometimes have to do hard things. They have to be brave.

Color the † beside times when you have to be brave.

✝ I tell the truth when I do something wrong.

✝ I stick up for someone who is being treated unfairly.

✝ I do not take something that is not mine.

✝ I am kind to someone who is unkind to me.

✝ I am a friend to someone who is unpopular.

Talk about the statements beside the crosses you have colored. Share them with a friend.

SHARING LIFE

Why does it take courage to be a disciple of Jesus?

How do you think Jesus helps us to have such courage?

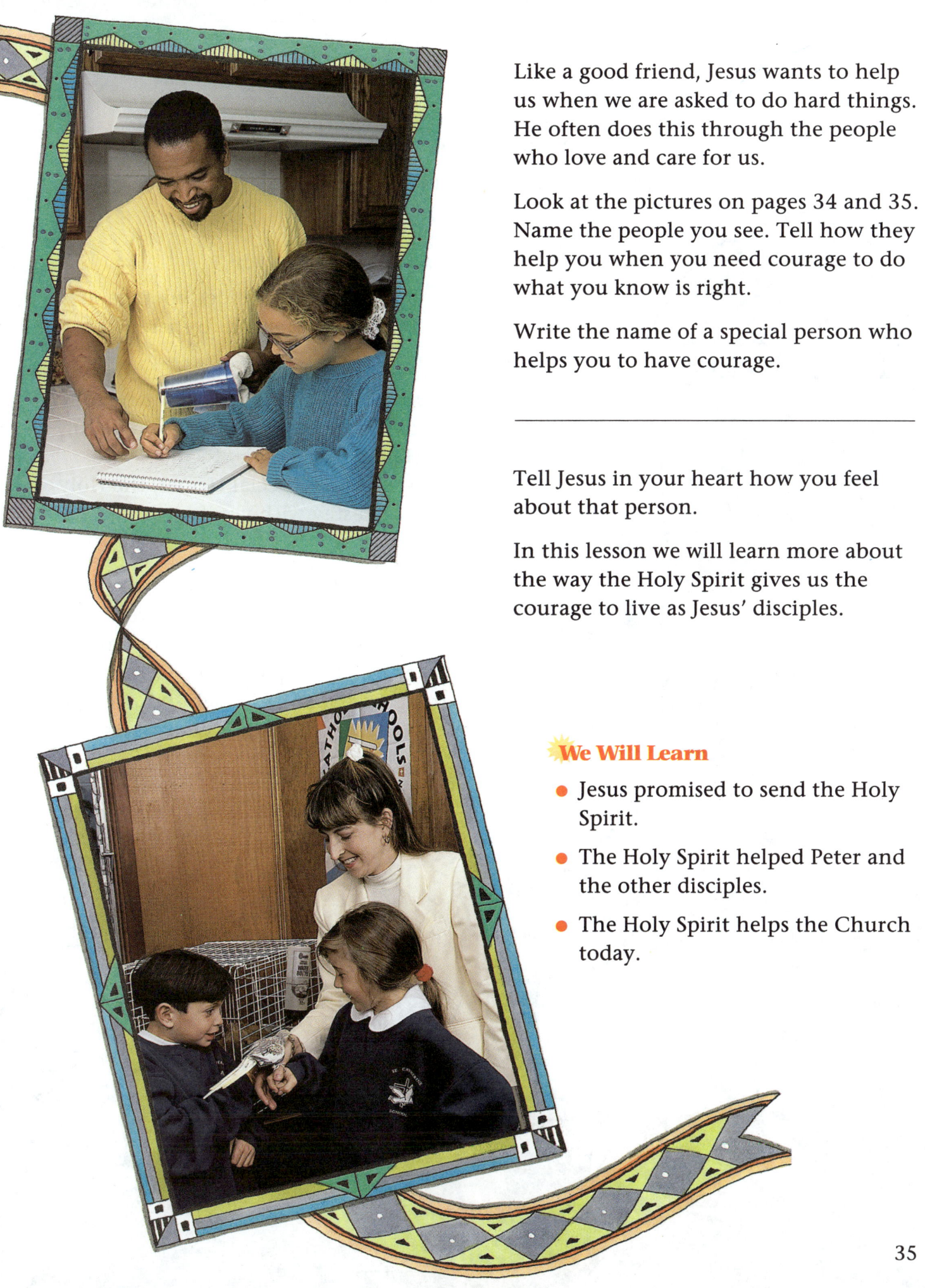

Like a good friend, Jesus wants to help us when we are asked to do hard things. He often does this through the people who love and care for us.

Look at the pictures on pages 34 and 35. Name the people you see. Tell how they help you when you need courage to do what you know is right.

Write the name of a special person who helps you to have courage.

_____

Tell Jesus in your heart how you feel about that person.

In this lesson we will learn more about the way the Holy Spirit gives us the courage to live as Jesus' disciples.

We Will Learn

- Jesus promised to send the Holy Spirit.
- The Holy Spirit helped Peter and the other disciples.
- The Holy Spirit helps the Church today.

Lord Jesus, help me to have the courage to do and say what I know is right.

Why is it sometimes hard to do what is right?

Jesus Promised a Helper

Jesus knew His disciples needed courage to be His faithful followers and to share His good news with everyone.

Jesus promised His disciples that when He returned to His Father, He would send them a special Helper. Jesus said, "I will ask the Father to send you a special Helper, the Holy Spirit, who will stay with you forever." From John 14:16

After Jesus ascended into heaven, His disciples stayed in Jerusalem. They were frightened without Jesus and did not have the courage to tell people about Him. They were afraid that they, too, might be arrested and put to death.

The Holy Spirit is God, the third Person of the Blessed Trinity.

The apostles and other disciples gathered together with Mary, the mother of Jesus, to pray and wait for the coming of the Holy Spirit.

Sometimes we may feel afraid, too. We want to be followers of Jesus, but it takes great courage.

Jesus sends the Holy Spirit to help us, too. The Holy Spirit gives us the courage to be brave and to live as disciples of Jesus. The Holy Spirit is God, the third Person of the Blessed Trinity. The Holy Spirit is our special Helper.

Complete this prayer to the Holy Spirit.

† God the Holy Spirit, help me to

_____

_____

_____

_____

Explain why the disciples of Jesus were afraid after He left them.

When will you ask the Holy Spirit to help you?

OUR CATHOLIC FAITH

■ God the Holy Spirit, help me to listen to Your word.

■ Whom do you help to do the right thing?

The Holy Spirit Came

It was a special day in Jerusalem. It was the feast when many Jewish people came to thank God for the first crops harvested from their fields.

Jesus' friends gathered to wait for the Helper whom Jesus had promised.

All at once, they heard a noise like a loud wind blowing. The disciples saw what looked like flames of fire in the air. It seemed as if the flames spread out and touched each person there. The disciples were all filled with the Holy Spirit.

Jesus' disciples were no longer afraid. They came out of the place where they were hiding and began to speak with courage to all the people.

Peter, the leader of Jesus' disciples, stood up and spoke to the people. He said, "What you now see and hear is Jesus' gift to us. Jesus has sent us the Holy Spirit."
From Acts of the Apostles 2:1–12, 33

We call this day the feast of Pentecost.

The Holy Spirit continues to help us today. Sometimes we may be afraid to live as followers of Jesus. The Holy Spirit gives us courage to say and to do the right thing as disciples of Jesus, especially when this is hard to do.

The Holy Spirit also helps us to love one another and to be peacemakers.

Pray the Glory to the Father on page 277.

Tell the story of what happened to Jesus' disciples on Pentecost.

How will you show that you have courage to say and do the right thing?

OUR CATHOLIC FAITH

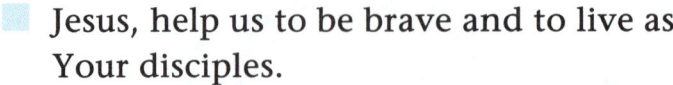

■ Jesus, help us to be brave and to live as Your disciples.

■ Tell how the Holy Spirit helps you today.

The Holy Spirit Helps the Church

Almost three thousand people were baptized on the feast of Pentecost.

Peter, the leader of the disciples, said to them, "Be baptized in the name of Jesus Christ, so that your sins will be forgiven; and you will receive God's gift, the Holy Spirit."
From Acts of the Apostles 2:38

Everyone who was baptized received the Holy Spirit. Sometimes we call this day the birthday of the Church.

The Holy Spirit continues to help the Church today. As members of the Church, we have been baptized and have received the Holy Spirit.

As Catholics, we believe that the Holy Spirit comes to us in a special way in the sacrament of Confirmation. When we are confirmed, the bishop or priest says, "Be sealed with the Gift of the Holy Spirit." This means that the Holy Spirit is with us and strengthens us to live our faith.

Many Languages, One Message

Today the Holy Spirit helps the Catholic Church continue the mission Jesus gave His apostles and disciples. The Church proclaims the good news of Jesus in every country on earth and in every language. For example, if you travel to Taiwan, you might hear the message of Jesus in Chinese. In Africa, you might hear it in Swahili or Zulu.

Even in our own country, we share the good news in different languages. Has your parish ever celebrated Mass in Spanish or German or Polish? Can you find out how many different languages are used at Mass in your diocese?

The Church wants us to celebrate the Mass and to pray in our own languages. But no matter how many languages we hear in the Church, the message of Jesus is always the same.

See if you can find out the word for *God* in one other language besides your own.

Learn by heart **Faith Summary**

- God the Holy Spirit is the third Person of the Blessed Trinity.

- The Holy Spirit came to the disciples on Pentecost.

- The Holy Spirit helps us to live as disciples of Jesus.

The banners say "The Lord be with you" in Spanish, Swahili, and Polish.

Coming to Faith

Retell the story of Pentecost in your own words.

Imagine you are one of the three thousand persons baptized on Pentecost. What do you see, hear, and experience?

Share with one another what you would say to Saint Peter.

What would you do next? Why?

Practicing Faith

Talk together about the help you and your friends need to be disciples of Jesus. Then write your own prayer to the Holy Spirit here.

✝ Holy Spirit, be with us.
Help us to follow Jesus by

_____.

Now gather in a prayer circle. Take turns reading your prayers. After each one all say "Amen!"

Talk with your teacher about ways you and your family can use the "Faith Alive" section. Perhaps you will pray your Holy Spirit prayer together this week.

42

REVIEW · TEST

Check the circle beside the correct answer.

1. The Helper that Jesus promised to send is the _____.

    ◯ Holy Spirit   ◯ pope   ◯ bishop

2. The Holy Spirit is God, the third Person of the _____.

    ◯ apostles   ◯ Church   ◯ Blessed Trinity

3. Everyone who is _____ receives the Holy Spirit.

    ◯ born   ◯ baptized   ◯ the right age

4. The Holy Spirit comes to us in a special way in the sacrament of _____.

    ◯ Reconciliation   ◯ Matrimony   ◯ Confirmation

5. How does the Holy Spirit help you?

_____

_____

FAITH ALIVE AT HOME AND IN THE PARISH

In this lesson your child learned that Jesus sent the Holy Spirit to His disciples on the first Pentecost. On that day the Church was born as a formal community of faith. Your child also learned that God the Holy Spirit, the third Person of the Blessed Trinity, helps us today. Talk with your child about the feast of Pentecost and the role of the Holy Spirit in our lives. It is the Holy Spirit who helps us to live our faith and prepares us to encounter the risen Christ.

† Prayer to the Holy Spirit

Ask the members of your family to think of something for which they need the Holy Spirit's help. (Examples: I need the Holy Spirit to help me to be kind to a bully at school; to be more patient with a coworker; to control my temper when I am tired or frustrated; to share my faith with a friend.) Together, say this prayer to the Holy Spirit.

Let us pray that we may be filled with the Holy Spirit.

Come, Holy Spirit, give us the courage we need to be disciples of Jesus.

Holy Spirit Poster

On a large sheet of paper print this prayer: "Holy Spirit, fill me with Your love and courage." Invite your child to make a decorative border around the prayer. Then pray the prayer together. Hang the poster in a prominent place to remind your family to pray each day to the Holy Spirit.

4   The Church Today

Jesus, help us
to work for
Your kingdom.

OUR LIFE

"Beth, keep your eye on the ball!"
yelled Lisa as the ball went right
by Beth into the net.

"I know what I'm doing!" Beth
yelled back. "I'm the most
important player on the team."

Everyone laughed. Beth stormed off.

Jason yelled, "Who needs
a goalie like you?"

But the rest of the team didn't
know what to do. Should they get
Beth back? Could someone else take
her place?

What do you think happened next?

What do you think it takes for a
group to work together?

SHARING LIFE

Take a shoe with shoelaces. Work with a
partner to tie one shoelace in a bow.
Each partner can use only one hand.

What did you learn about teamwork?

Why is it sometimes hard to work
together as a team?

How does Jesus want us to work together
in His Church?

Read this recipe for good teamwork.

A Teamwork Recipe

Start with cooperation.
Add listening and helping.
Stir in respect and caring.
Mix together. Serves us all.

Now join with a partner to write a recipe for helping your group work together as one.

Our Recipe for Good Teamwork

Start with _____

Add _____

Stir in _____

Mix together. Serves us all.

Share your recipe with your group.

In this lesson we will learn about working together in the Church.

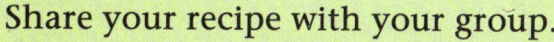

We Will Learn

- The Church is the body of Christ.
- The Church carries on the mission of Jesus.
- Our leaders help us in the Church.

45

Jesus, help us to work together as Your friends.

What happens when everyone does his or her part?

The Body of Christ

Jesus wants all His disciples to work together. Everyone has a part to play in the Church as we carry on Jesus' mission. One of Jesus' greatest disciples, Paul, taught the people what it meant to be a member of the Church.

Paul told the people that the Church was like a body. Each of our bodies has a head, hands, feet, nose, eyes, ears, and so on. Every part of a person's body is important.

So it is in the Church, the body of Christ. Everyone in the Church is an important part, or member, of the body of Christ. We are to work together, just like the many parts of a body.

Paul explained it this way: Christ is like one body that has many parts. Each part needs the others. If the foot were to say, "Because I am not a hand, I don't belong to the body," it would still be part of the body.

The eye cannot say to the hand, "I don't need you!" The head cannot say to the feet, "Well, I don't need you!" All the parts of the body need one another.

Paul ended his beautiful description of the Church by saying, "So, all of you are Christ's body, and each one is a part of it."

From 1 Corinthians 12:12–27

In the Church we work together with Jesus Christ as our Head.

Just as each part of the human body has something special to do, so each of us has something important to do in the Church. With the help of the Holy Spirit, each of us can do his or her part.

Circle one of the pictures on this page. Tell what part each person has in the Church, the body of Christ.

■ What do we mean when we say that the Church is the body of Christ?

■ What part will you play in the Church?

OUR CATHOLIC FAITH

■ Jesus, help us to bring the good news of Your love to all people.

■ Why do we all need to do our part in the Church?

The Mission of Jesus

Jesus' friends knew that God had given Jesus a very special mission. He was to bring about God's kingdom.

This means that Jesus was to tell the good news of God's love for all people. He was to show them how to do God's will by living with love, justice, and peace.

Jesus chose Peter to be the leader of His community, the Church. Peter led the other apostles and disciples as they carried on Jesus' mission. They spread the good news of Jesus all over the world. They lived it, too, by following the example of Jesus.

Today, the Church still continues the mission of Jesus. The Church teaches what Jesus taught. We are led by the successors of Peter and the apostles, our pope and bishops. All people are welcomed into Jesus' community, the Church. As the Church, we pray and worship God and serve others. God works through the Church to bring about the kingdom, or reign, of God.

The **pope** is the successor of Saint Peter and the leader of the whole Catholic Church.

We are the Church today. We are the body of Christ in the world. Together we carry on the mission of Jesus under the guidance of the Holy Spirit. Each of us has a part to play in bringing about the kingdom of God.

Here are some things we can do:

- Share with others the good news of Jesus by what we say and do.

- Pray and worship together, especially at Mass.

- Try to help others, especially those most in need.

Write a prayer to use this week, asking Jesus to help you carry out His mission.

_____

_____

_____

_____

- How does the Church continue Jesus' mission?

- What will you do to bring the good news to others?

49

OUR CATHOLIC FAITH

■ Take turns telling Jesus how you will be an active member of His Church.

■ Why does the Church need leaders?

Leaders in the Church Today

The people chosen to lead us in the Catholic Church are called *ministers*. *Minister* means "one who serves." Our ministers serve the Church and help us to work together. They lead us in worshiping God and caring for others.

The pope, the bishop of Rome, carries on the leadership work of Peter. He is the leader of the whole Catholic Church. The pope and bishops teach, guide, and sanctify, or make holy, the whole Church. They serve all members of the Church and help us to work together.

In our parishes other ordained ministers help us. Our priests lead us in prayer and worship. Our deacons help the priests at Mass and work with people in need.

Parishes have other ministers, too. Religious sisters, brothers, and lay ministers join all of us in working for justice and peace. Some teach; others help the sick and needy.

All of us are called by God to work together in the Church.

The Bishop of Our Diocese

Our bishop is the leader of all the Catholic parishes in our diocese. He has a big responsibility in caring for many people. He carries on the work of the first apostles. When the bishop visits a parish to celebrate the liturgy, he dresses in a special way. He wears a mitre on his head and a special ring on his finger. In his hand he carries a long staff called a crosier.

The crosier is shaped like a shepherd's crook. It reminds us that our bishop is the shepherd, the chief teacher, and the pastor of our diocese. Like Jesus, the Good Shepherd, he leads us and helps us to work together as a community of Jesus' disciples.

We pray for our bishop at every Mass. When you hear the bishop's name mentioned at Mass, will you remember to pray for him?

Learn by heart **Faith Summary**

- The Church carries on the mission of Jesus Christ.

- Our pope, bishops, priests, and deacons are the ordained ministers of the Church.

- All Church members have a part to play in bringing about the kingdom of God.

51

Coming To Faith

Talk to one another and share what you know about:

- the mission of Jesus.
- the mission of the Church today.
- our mission as third graders.

Practicing Faith

Be faith-filled members of the Church! Your mission is to decide how you can:

- tell others about Jesus.
- pray and worship together, especially at Mass.
- try to help others, especially those most in need.

Share your ideas. Then decide on something to do together as a group.

Talk with your teacher about ways you and your family might use the "Faith Alive" section. You might want to ask family members to do the Body of Christ activity with you.

REVIEW · TEST

Check the circle beside the correct answer.

1. The _____ is the body of Christ in the world.

◯ Law of Love   ◯ Church   ◯ kingdom of God

2. All bishops, priests, and deacons receive the sacrament of _____.

◯ Anointing   ◯ Matrimony   ◯ Holy Orders

3. The Church carries on the mission of _____.

◯ the pope   ◯ Jesus   ◯ lay ministers

4. All Church members are to help bring about the _____.

◯ end of the world   ◯ resurrection   ◯ kingdom of God

5. How can you help carry on the mission of Jesus?

_____

_____

FAITH ALIVE   AT HOME AND IN THE PARISH

In this lesson your child learned one important image of the Church—that the Church is the body of Christ. Your child also learned that each member of Christ's body shares in Jesus' mission of helping to bring about the kingdom, or reign, of God. Talk with your child about the importance of telling others about Jesus, of praying and worshiping together, and of trying to help those in need. The following activities may help you emphasize how each person in your family can contribute to the mission of Jesus.

We Are the Body of Christ

Discuss ways each family member can help the Church bring the good news of God's love to others. Have each person decide on one good thing to do this week to show that she or he is part of the body of Christ.

The Good Things We Do

On a large piece of paper write the names of the persons in your family. Invite each family member to list their gifts and talents, the good things he or she knows how to do. Then have them add to one another's lists, noting other good qualities of each member of the family. Talk about ways these gifts and talents can be used to carry on the mission of Jesus.

5   Our Parish Church

Dear God, help
our parish to
live as Your
people.

Our Life

Father Martin asked Carmen, Steve,
Nicky, and Lauren to give a tour of the
church to the third graders from the
nearby Baptist church. During the tour,
the children explained some of what
you see in this picture.

CANDLES

CRUCIFIX

PRESIDER'S
CHAIR

AMBO
(LECTERN)

PLACE
OF THE
ASSEMBLY

ALTAR

BAPTISMAL
FONT
OR POOL

Act out the visit. Choose people to be
Carmen, Steve, Nicky and Lauren. The rest
are the visitors who ask questions about
each thing in church.

Sharing Life

What do you like best about your parish
community and its church? What more do
you want to learn?

Work with a friend to design a banner about your parish church. On the banner, thank God for something you like about your parish community. Decorate your banner.

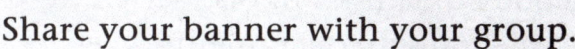

Share your banner with your group.

In this lesson we will discover how our parish tries to live as a loving community of Jesus' disciples.

We Will Learn

- We belong to a parish.
- Our parish church is a holy place.
- We pray and worship God in our parish church.

■ Begin today's lesson by praying the Morning Offering. (See page 278.)

■ When do you pray with other people? Tell about one of those times.

We Belong to a Parish

Catholics come together to pray with other people in their parish. A parish is a group of Jesus' friends who worship God together. Each parish is usually named after God, Mary, or a saint.

In a parish there are young people and old people, single people and married people. There are rich people and poor people. There are people of different races and backgrounds.

Everyone should feel at home in our Catholic parishes. One thing that the word *catholic* means is that everyone is welcome.

Our parish is our special home in the Church, the body of Christ. In our parish we pray and we celebrate the sacraments. We help one another to live as disciples of Jesus.

We try to build a loving Catholic community. When other people come to our parish, they should be able to say of us, "See how these Christians love one another."

Each parish has a special building called the parish church. This is our worship space. It is a holy place where we pray and worship God as a parish family, especially at Mass on Sunday or on Saturday evening.

Besides going to Mass on Sundays, we also go to our parish church to celebrate many great feast days. On these days, we remember special moments in the lives of Jesus, Mary, and the saints.

Write the name of your parish.

_____

_____

■ Describe what we do together in our parish church.

■ What will you do to help make your parish a loving community?

OUR CATHOLIC FAITH

sanctuary lamp

tabernacle

- Begin by praying together the vocation prayer on page 278.

- Tell about some things that make your parish church a special place.

Our Parish Church

When we enter the church, there is a basin with holy water near the door. We take some holy water on our fingers and make the sign of the cross to remind us of our Baptism. We *genuflect* toward the tabernacle to show respect for Jesus present in the Blessed Sacrament. This means we bend our right knee to the floor.

In our church there is an altar, or table. The altar is in the sanctuary, the part of the church building where the priest leads us in worshiping God. At Mass we bring our gifts to the altar.

A crucifix and lighted candles are near the altar when we worship God together. A crucifix is a cross that reminds us that Jesus died and rose to bring us new life.

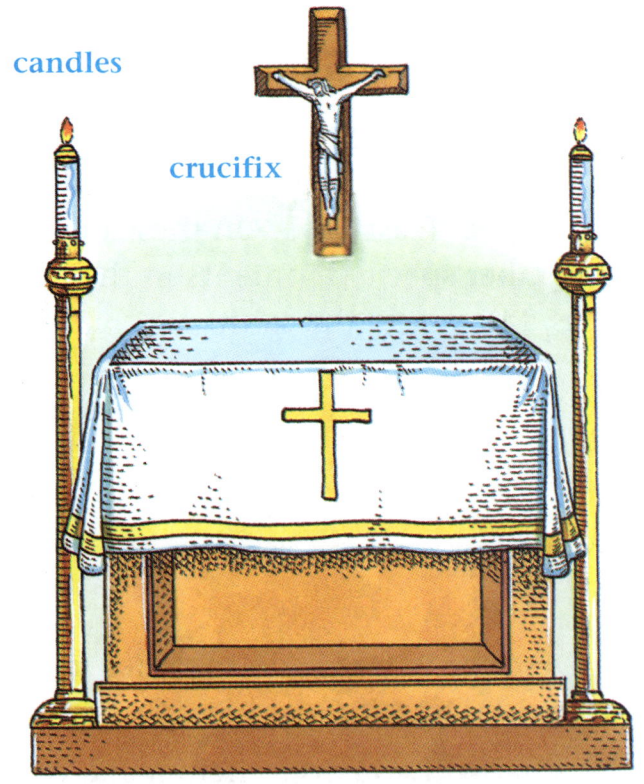

candles

crucifix

altar

Blessed Sacrament is another name for the Eucharist. Jesus is really present in the Blessed Sacrament.

Near the altar there is an ambo (lectern). Here the word of God is read to us.

The paschal candle is a large candle. It is lit during the Easter season to remind us that Jesus is risen from the dead and is always with us.

Somewhere in each parish church there is a baptismal font or small baptismal pool. This is where people are baptized and welcomed into the Church as members of the body of Christ.

When we look around our parish church, we may see statues of Jesus, or of Mary, Joseph, and the other saints. Our church windows are often made of beautiful stained glass. They tell stories about Jesus and the saints.

The tabernacle is the place in our church where the Blessed Sacrament is kept. A sanctuary lamp burns near the tabernacle to remind us that Jesus is really present.

Pray and color this prayer we can say when we visit Jesus present in the Blessed Sacrament.

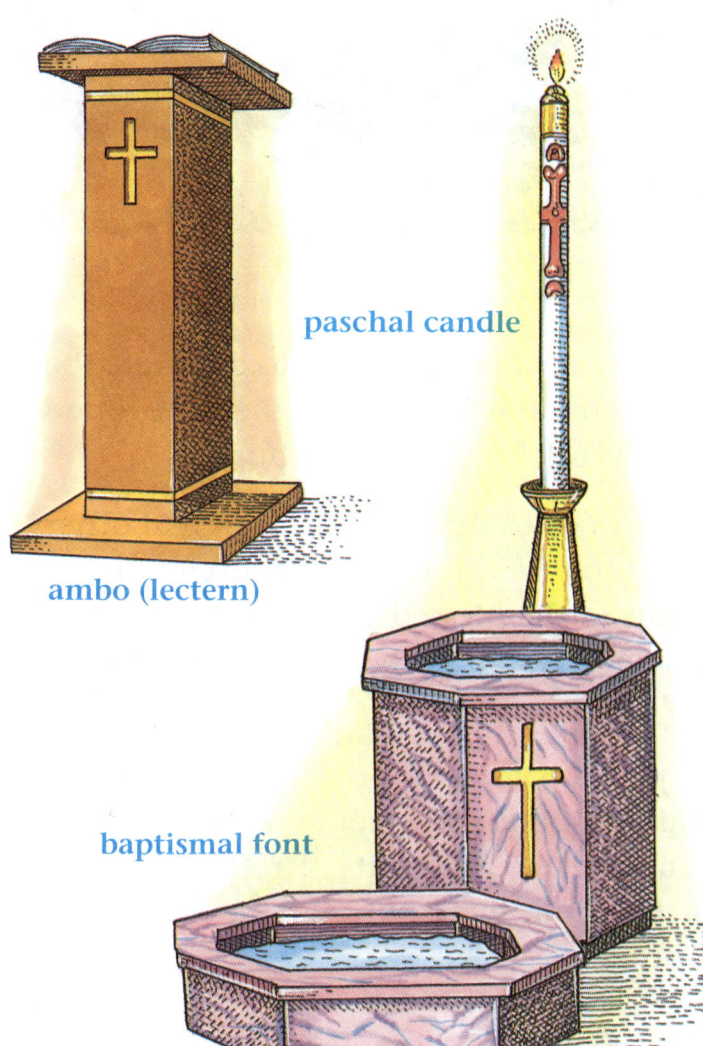

paschal candle

ambo (lectern)

baptismal font

Jesus,

thank You for being here
in my parish church
where I can visit You.

■ What are some things we see in our parish church?

■ When will you visit your church? Why?

OUR CATHOLIC FAITH

- Together pray the "Glory to the Father." (See page 277.)

- What is your favorite part of your parish church? Why?

Worship in Our Parish

Sunday is our special day to worship God. We take part in the Mass every Sunday or Saturday evening in our parish church. We also gather to worship God at Mass on six special days called holy days of obligation.

We go to our parish church to celebrate the sacraments. When someone dies, the funeral service is celebrated in our church.

Catholics go to their parish church at other times, too. We can visit our church to pray to Jesus in the Blessed Sacrament. We can tell Jesus what is in our hearts. Jesus is present and listening to us.

Our parish is much more than a church building. It is all the people who belong to our parish community. Together we worship God, share our faith, and show love for others.

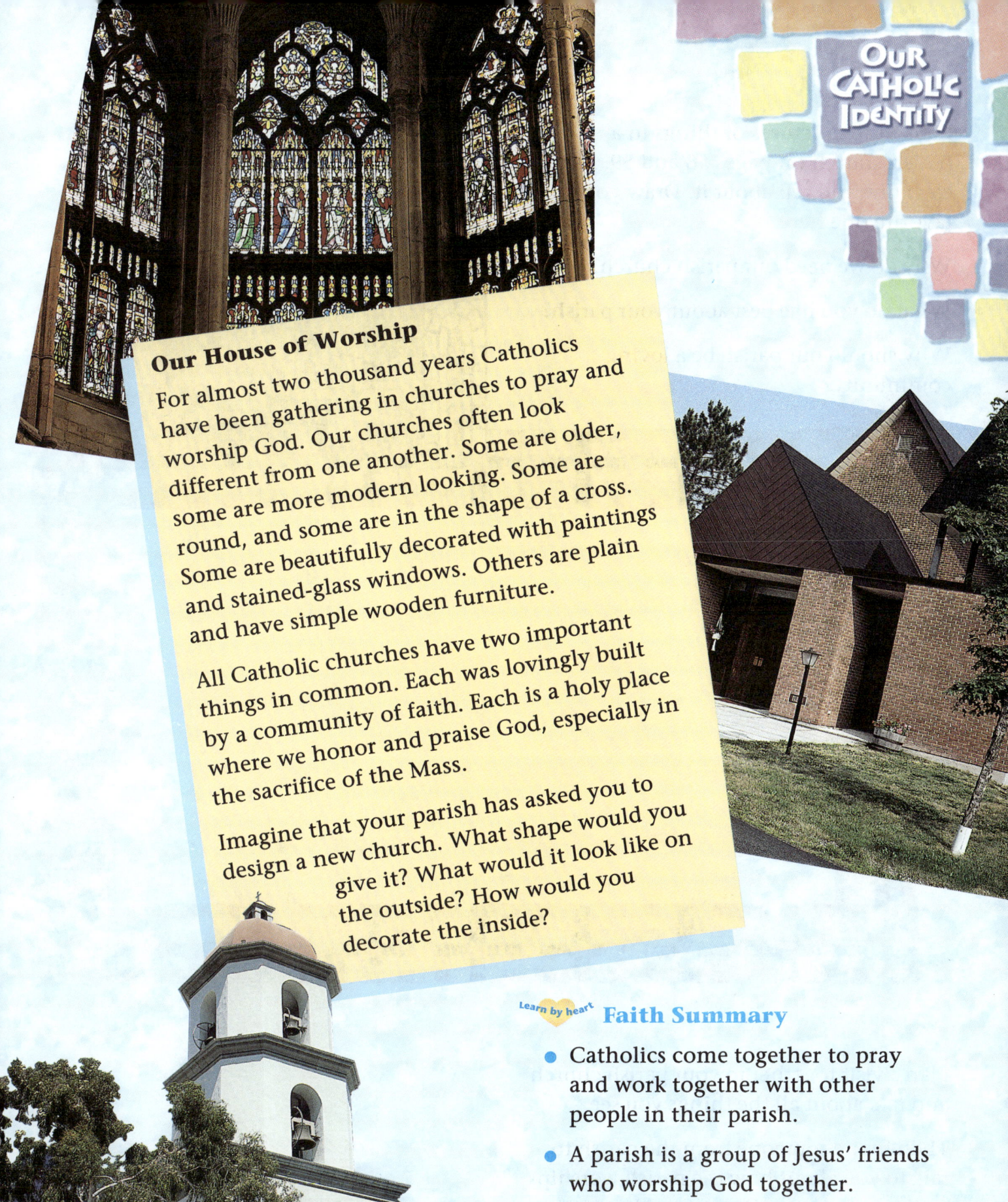

Our House of Worship

For almost two thousand years Catholics have been gathering in churches to pray and worship God. Our churches often look different from one another. Some are older, some are more modern looking. Some are round, and some are in the shape of a cross. Some are beautifully decorated with paintings and stained-glass windows. Others are plain and have simple wooden furniture.

All Catholic churches have two important things in common. Each was lovingly built by a community of faith. Each is a holy place where we honor and praise God, especially in the sacrifice of the Mass.

Imagine that your parish has asked you to design a new church. What shape would you give it? What would it look like on the outside? How would you decorate the inside?

Learn by heart **Faith Summary**

- Catholics come together to pray and work together with other people in their parish.

- A parish is a group of Jesus' friends who worship God together.

- Our parish church is a holy place where we pray and worship God.

61

Coming To Faith

Look at the pictures of things in a parish church on pages 58 and 59. Name each one and tell about it. Draw your favorite one here.

Why do we need our parish church?

What do you like best about your parish?

Why should our parish be a loving community?

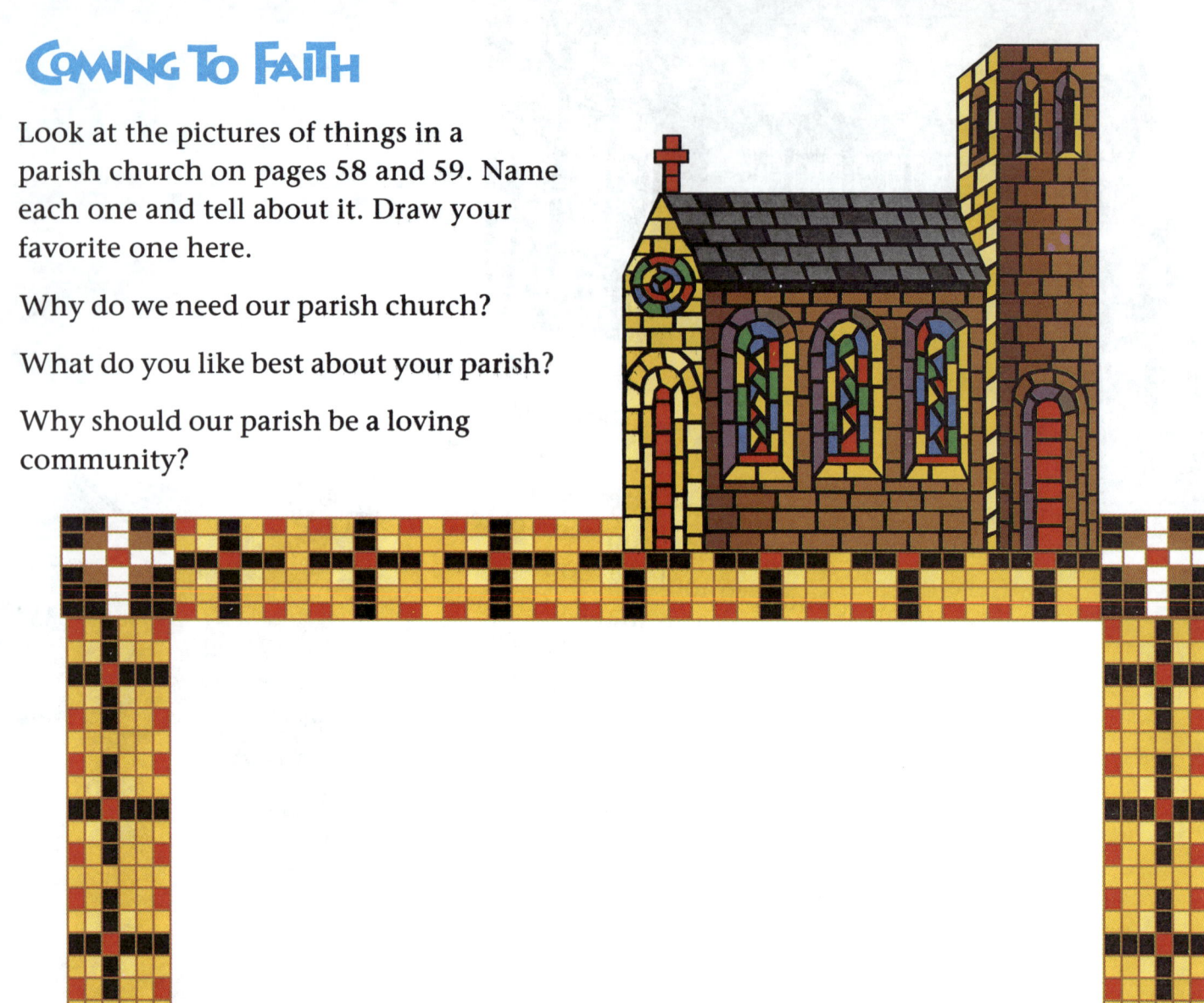

Practicing Faith

Plan a visit together to your parish church and talk about all the things you see.

Then invite someone from the parish to talk to you about how the parish worships God and cares for those in need.
How will your group share in this work?

Talk with your teacher about ways you and your family might use the "Faith Alive" section. You might plan with your family a visit to the Blessed Sacrament in your parish church.

REVIEW ■ TEST

Circle **True** or **False**. If you are not sure, circle **?**.

1. A parish is a group of Jesus' friends who worship God together.   **True**   **False**   **?**

2. Our parish church is a community of Jesus' disciples.   **True**   **False**   **?**

3. We go to our parish church to celebrate Mass and the sacraments.   **True**   **False**   **?**

4. Our parish is all the people who belong to our parish community.   **True**   **False**   **?**

5. Write how you can help your parish to be a loving community.

_____

_____

_____

_____

FAITH ALIVE AT HOME AND IN THE PARISH

In this lesson your child learned about our parish community and its church. Talk with your child about ways our parish helps one another to live as Jesus' disciples by worshiping God together, by sharing our faith, and by showing love for others, especially people in need. You may want to use the following activities to help your child appreciate the parish church as our holy place of prayer and worship.

Know Your Parish Church

Write the words listed below on slips of paper. Place them in a box or a small paper bag. Have each person in your family choose one slip of paper, say the word or words aloud, and tell something about it.

altar	crucifix	baptismal font
candles	tabernacle	lectern
statue	sanctuary	stained-glass window

Visit to the Blessed Sacrament

Take time to visit Jesus in the Blessed Sacrament with your family. Spend a few minutes in quiet prayer together. Remind your family that we genuflect before the tabernacle to show our reverence for Jesus who is present in the Blessed Sacrament. Point out that we also show respect in church by being quiet, except for the times we pray or sing together.

6 | Reconciliation

Our Life

Here is a riddle for you to solve.

When somebody hurts me,
When I am sad and blue,
It helps to hear three little words
To make me smile for you.

And when I hurt another,
I know just what to say—
Three little words we know so well
Can chase the hurt away.

Write the three little words in each speech balloon.

Tell about a time a person said these words to you.

Sharing Life

What do you think the world would be like:
- if everyone felt sorry for doing wrong;
- if everyone said they were sorry;
- if everyone tried to do better?

Share how you feel when someone you love forgives you.

64

With a friend, decorate the patchwork banner. Use words and pictures that tell what the world would be like if everyone felt sorry for doing wrong.

- What words might you use?

- What pictures might you draw?

Share your banner with your friends.

In this lesson we will learn more about God's forgiveness.

We Will Learn

- We celebrate God's love and forgiveness of our sins in the sacrament of Reconciliation.

- In the sacrament of Reconciliation we receive the forgiveness of God and are reconciled with the Church.

OUR CATHOLIC FAITH

We Tell God We Are Sorry

When we sin and are sorry, God forgives us. The Church helps us to celebrate God's love and the forgiveness of our sins in the sacrament of Reconciliation. In this sacrament we praise and thank God for God's great love.

In this sacrament, we receive the forgiveness of God and are reconciled with the Church. We try to begin again to love God and others as we should.

When we celebrate the sacrament of Reconciliation, we follow these five steps.

1. We think about the times we made bad choices and did not follow the Ten Commandments or the Law of Love. We call this our examination of conscience.

2. We meet with the priest and tell him our sins. We call this confession.

3. The priest gives us a penance. A penance is something good we do or prayers we say to show God we are sorry and will try to do better.

4. We say a special prayer to say "I'm sorry." We call it the Act of Contrition.

5. The priest says the words of absolution. These words tell us that God has really forgiven us through the ministry of the Church.

COMING TO FAITH

How does the Church help us to say "I am sorry"?

Work with a partner to practice the steps we follow in celebrating the sacrament of Reconciliation.

Practicing Faith

Celebrating Forgiveness Together

Sing as an opening prayer.

♫ Amazing grace, how sweet the sound
That saved and set me free.
I once was lost but now I'm found;
Was blind but now I see. ♫

Leader: Loving God, we come to
You to say that we are sorry for the times
we have not lived the Ten Commandments
and the Law of Love.

Reading: John 15:9–14

Leader: Let us take a few minutes to
think about the times we have not
loved God and others as Jesus taught
us. (Pause)

All: (Say an Act of Contrition. See page 277.)

Leader: Loving God, we know that when we
are truly sorry, You forgive us. You
always love us. Help us to love and
forgive one another.

Let us be very still for a moment. Then
thank God for God's gifts
of forgiveness and love.

Sing as a closing prayer.

♫ Through many dangers, toils, and snares
We have already come.
'Tis grace that brought me safe this far,
And grace will lead me home. ♫

Talk with your teacher about ways
you and your family might use the
"Faith Alive" section. You might plan
with your family a peace conference
and prayer.

REVIEW ■ TEST

When we celebrate the sacrament of Reconciliation, we follow five steps. Put the steps below in the right order. Number the steps 1, 2, 3, 4, and 5. Which comes first? second? and so on?

_____ The priest says the words of absolution. These words tell us that God has really forgiven us through the ministry of the Church.

_____ We meet with the priest and tell him our sins. We call this confession.

_____ We say a special prayer to tell God "I am sorry." We call it the Act of Contrition.

_____ We think about the times we made bad choices and did not follow the Ten Commandments or the Law of Love. We call this our examination of conscience.

_____ The priest gives us a penance. A penance is something good we do or prayers we say to show God we are sorry and will try to do better.

FAITH ALIVE AT HOME AND IN THE PARISH

In this lesson your child learned more about the sacrament of Reconciliation. Talk with your child about God's readiness to forgive us when we are sorry for the hurtful things we said or did. You might also want to help your child learn by heart the five steps for celebrating the sacrament of Reconciliation. (See page 66.)

Many children (and adults) think that by looking appropriately woeful and muttering the words "I am sorry" all can be forgiven. However, repentance also entails a new effort to do better, to change our ways. The Catholic Church clearly teaches that whenever we do a serious wrong to someone, we must try to make reparation.

Talk About Forgiveness

Discuss with your child the importance of asking forgiveness when we hurt someone. Then talk about why we must be ready to forgive those who have hurt us.

† Family Prayer

At bedtime, encourage your child to join you in saying an Act of Contrition. (See page 277.)

Celebrate Reconciliation Together

The next time your parish has a communal celebration of the sacrament of Reconciliation, invite your child to participate in it with you.

Learn by heart ## Faith Summary

- We celebrate God's love and forgiveness of our sins in the sacrament of Reconciliation.

- In the sacrament of Reconciliation we receive the forgiveness of God and are reconciled with the Church.

7 Eucharist

Jesus, thank
You for being
our Bread
of Life.

OUR LIFE

After Jesus rose from the dead, He stayed with His disciples for forty days. Then the time came for Him to return to His Father. Jesus knew that His friends would miss Him very much when He was gone. So He gathered them together and told them to go through the whole world and tell the good news to all people. Then He made this wonderful promise. He said, "I will be with you always, to the end of the world."
From Matthew 28:20

What do you hear Jesus saying with these words?

When do you most feel that Jesus is with you?

SHARING LIFE

Close your eyes. Think about Jesus' promise. How does it make you feel to know that Jesus is always with you? Share your feelings together.

Sometimes we can show our feelings through colors.

Name a color you might use to show:

- you are happy;

- you are sad.

Tell why you chose each color.

Now make a drawing. Use colors to show how you feel about Jesus' promise to be with you always.

Share your picture with your group. Ask them to guess why you chose the colors you did. If you have another reason for choosing a color, explain your reason to the group.

In this lesson we will learn about a special way that Jesus is with us.

We Will Learn

- Jesus gave us the gift of Himself in the Eucharist at the Last Supper.

- The Mass is both a meal and a sacrifice.

OUR CATHOLIC FAITH

We Celebrate Eucharist

At the Last Supper, Jesus gave us the gift of Himself in the Eucharist. The Mass is our celebration of the Eucharist. At Mass we remember the Last Supper and Jesus' sacrifice on the cross for us. That is why the Eucharist is both a meal and a sacrifice. Together we share the gift of Jesus' real presence with us.

Let us prepare a celebration of the Eucharist.

1. Write a letter inviting your pastor to celebrate the Mass with your group.

2. Have a special reason or intention for celebrating this Mass.

3. Look up the readings for the Mass. Choose readers. Practice the readings.

4. Keeping these readings in mind, decide on songs or hymns for the Mass. Practice them ahead of time.

5. Decide who will be altar servers and who will bring the gifts of bread and wine to the altar.

6. Think about or write some petitions for the Prayer of the Faithful. These should ask God for what we need for the Church, the world, and ourselves. Those who will read the petitions should practice them.

7. Make up a prayer to say together after Communion. This prayer should tell God how we will try as a group to help those in need of our love and care.

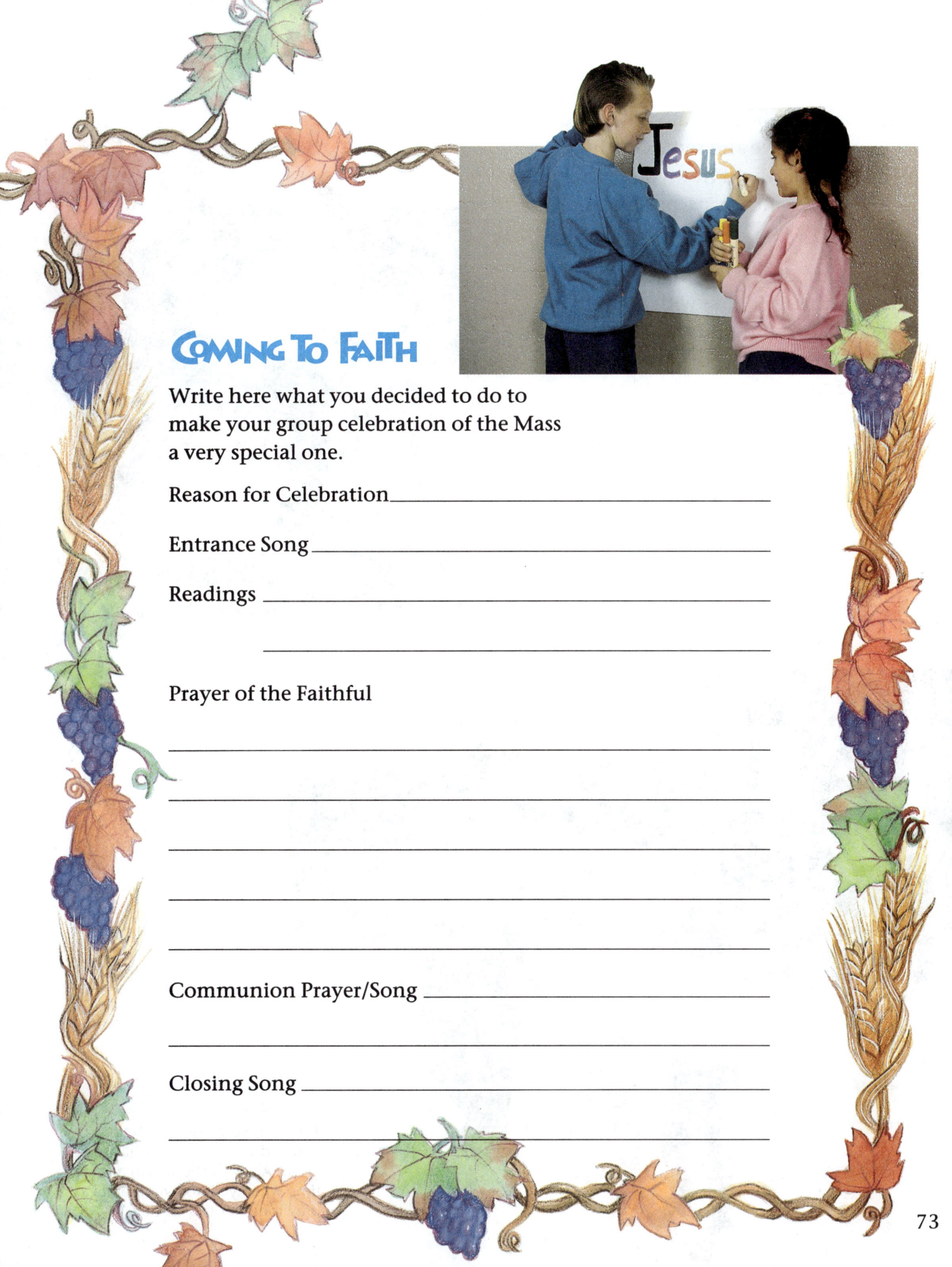

COMING TO FAITH

Write here what you decided to do to
make your group celebration of the Mass
a very special one.

Reason for Celebration _____

Entrance Song _____

Readings _____

_____

Prayer of the Faithful

_____

_____

_____

_____

Communion Prayer/Song _____

_____

Closing Song _____

_____

PRACTICING FAITH

Talk together about what you will do this week to love and serve God in others. Think about how you are helping others experience Jesus' presence in the world.

Write your ideas in the space provided. Then exchange books with your friends. Read what your friends have written. Encourage them to put their ideas into practice.

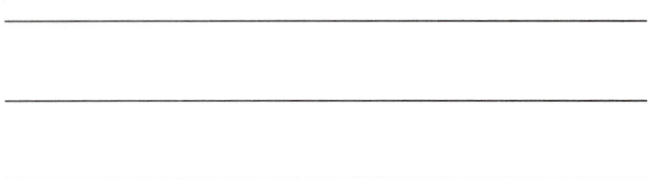

_____

_____

_____

Talk with your teacher about ways you and your family might use the "Faith Alive" section. Plan a special time when you and your family can pray together this week.

REVIEW • TEST

Circle **True** or **False**.

If you are not sure, circle **?**.

1. Jesus gave us the gift of Himself in the Eucharist. **True** **False** **?**

2. At Mass we remember the Last Supper and Jesus' sacrifice on the cross. **True** **False** **?**

3. The Eucharist is both a meal and a sacrifice. **True** **False** **?**

4. Write what you will say to Jesus when you receive Him in Holy Communion.

_____

_____

_____

_____

FAITH ALIVE AT HOME AND IN THE PARISH

In this lesson your child participated in planning a special group celebration of the Mass. Ask him or her to tell you about the plans for the celebration. (See pages 72–73.)

It is also important for children to develop an appreciation of the Eucharist as something shared, something we do as a community. The Acts of the Apostles tells us that the early Christians spent their time "learning from the apostles, taking part in fellowship, and sharing in the fellowship meals and prayers" (Acts 2:42). All goods were held in common, and everyone was provided for according to need. The sharing and nourishment of the Eucharist led to a life shared in mutual concern and service. The same should be true for us today.

Help your child grow in appreciation of the Eucharist as our communal celebration of Christ's special meal and sacrifice by worshiping together with your parish each week. It is so important for children to learn to fulfill every Catholic's serious obligation to participate in the Mass each weekend.

† Family Prayer

With your family make up a short prayer to thank Jesus for the gift of the Mass. Pray your family prayer together.

Learn by heart ### Faith Summary

- Jesus gave us the gift of Himself in the Eucharist at the Last Supper.

- The Mass is both a meal and a sacrifice.

8 Our Parish Prays

Jesus, teach us to pray.

Our Life

Here is a story from the Bible.

Jesus and His disciples went to visit Martha and Mary, who were friends of Jesus. They welcomed Jesus into their home. Mary was so happy to see Jesus that she sat at His feet to hear His words. Martha was upset over all the work she had to do, so she went to Jesus and said, "Lord, don't you care that my sister has left me to do all the work by myself? Tell her to come and help me!"

Jesus said, "Martha, Martha! You are worried about so many things. Just one thing is needed. Mary has chosen the best thing of all."
From Luke 10:38–42

What had Mary chosen to do?

What do you think Mary heard Jesus say as she listened to His words?

Sharing Life

When do you listen to and talk to Jesus?

What are some things that worry you most?

How can Jesus help you when you worry?

List some things people do when they are worried.

_____

_____

_____

_____

Go over your list. Do you think any of these things help people with their worries? How should our faith help us to deal with our worries? Share your thoughts with your group.

Think about the story of Mary and Martha. Tell what advice you think they might give to a disciple of Jesus who is worried.

In this lesson we will learn how prayer can help us, not just when we are worried, but all the time.

We Will Learn

- We can pray alone or with others.
- We pray to the Blessed Virgin Mary and to the other saints.
- We pray for the living and the dead.

OUR CATHOLIC FAITH

- Act out the story of Martha and Mary.

- What do you think people your age say to God when they pray?

Prayer Alone and with Others

Prayer is talking and listening to God. We can talk to God using our own words, or we can say prayers that all Catholics pray.

We pray for many reasons:

- We can praise God, who made us.

- We can tell God we are sorry for something we have done wrong.

- We can ask God's help for all people.

- We can ask God's help for our own needs.

- We can thank God for God's love and care.

We can pray at any time. In the morning we can offer God all the things we will do that day. We can say this prayer.

✝ A Morning Offering

O loving God, I give You this day
All that I think and do and say,
Uniting it with what was done
On earth, by Jesus Christ, Your Son.

At night we can thank God for being with us all day. We can say this prayer.

✝ An Evening Prayer

Dear God, before I fall asleep
I want to thank You for this day,
so full of Your kindness and Your love.
I close my eyes to rest now,
safe in Your loving care.

God also wants us to pray as a parish community. We pray with our parish when we celebrate Mass and the other sacraments together.

We know Jesus is present with us when we gather with others to pray. He told His disciples, "Where two or three come together in My name, I am there with them."
From Matthew 18:20

▪ When will you talk and listen to God this week?

▪ Thank You, God, for being with me when I pray.

OUR CATHOLIC FAITH

■ Lord Jesus, teach us to pray.

■ Do you know someone who loves God very much? How does he or she show it?

Mary and the Saints

Saints are people who loved God very much. They tried to do God's will during their lives on earth. Now they are happy with God forever in heaven.

Saint Thérèse of Lisieux
(at age 11)

Saint John Bosco

We know that everyone in the Church is united by Baptism in the one body of Christ. This includes even those who have died. So the saints are our brothers and sisters in faith. We have a special bond with them. They pray to God for us.

We should learn about the saints so that we can try to live as they did. We can pray to the saints for the help we need to follow Jesus better.

During their lives on earth, the saints were people like us. Because they are now with God forever, they can help us to love God and others as they did.

Some saints have been chosen by the Church to be canonized. In a special way they show us how to live holy lives. But on November 1, our parish remembers everyone in heaven. We celebrate the feast of All Saints.

The Blessed Virgin Mary is a very special saint. She is the greatest of all the disciples of Jesus. As the mother of Jesus, she is the Mother of God and our mother, too. Mary prays for each of us and helps us to be disciples of Jesus.

Mary has a special love for the poor and for people treated unfairly. In our country, we celebrate many feast days in honor of Mary.

Saint Joseph is a special saint, too. He was the husband of Mary and the foster father of Jesus. Saint Joseph loved and cared for Jesus and Mary. Catholics have a special love for Saint Joseph. We call him the patron saint of the whole Church.

Blessed Virgin Mary

FAITH WORD

Canonized means being named a saint by the Church.

Saint Joseph

Name and write about your favorite saint.

_____

_____

_____

_____

_____

_____

- Using your own words, describe what a saint is.
- What saint will you ask to help you today?

OUR CATHOLIC FAITH

- Sing "Amazing Grace" from page 68.
- Tell about someone you know who has died. Remember to pray for that person.

Prayer for the Living and the Dead

When someone we have known and loved dies, we are sad. We miss that person very much. But we believe that God has given each of us a life that lasts forever. We hope that some day we will all be together again with God in heaven.

All the members of the Church, living and dead, are united by Baptism. This is what we mean by the communion of saints. This bond of unity is not broken even by death. This is why we pray for those who have died. On November 2, the feast of All Souls, we pray for all the dead that they may rest in God's peace forever.

All the friends of Jesus, whether living or dead, can still help one another. We can pray for one another every day. A special time to pray for those who have died is at Mass.

A Wonderful Way to Pray

The Catholic Church has a tradition of remembering a particular person at Mass. We call this the Mass intention.

In your parish bulletin, you may see a list of Masses with a person's name next to the time of each Mass. This means that the person named will be remembered and prayed for at that Mass.

Members of your parish may ask the priest to offer a Mass for a loved one on the anniversary of that person's death. They may also request that a Mass be offered for someone who is ill or for a couple celebrating a wedding anniversary.

The Mass intention is a wonderful way for our parish community to pray for one of its members, living or dead.

Perhaps members of your family may want to have a Mass offered for someone you love. If they do, try to go to the Mass together.

Learn by heart **Faith Summary**

- Prayer is talking and listening to God.
- We ask the Blessed Virgin Mary and the other saints to pray for us.
- By Baptism we belong to the communion of saints.

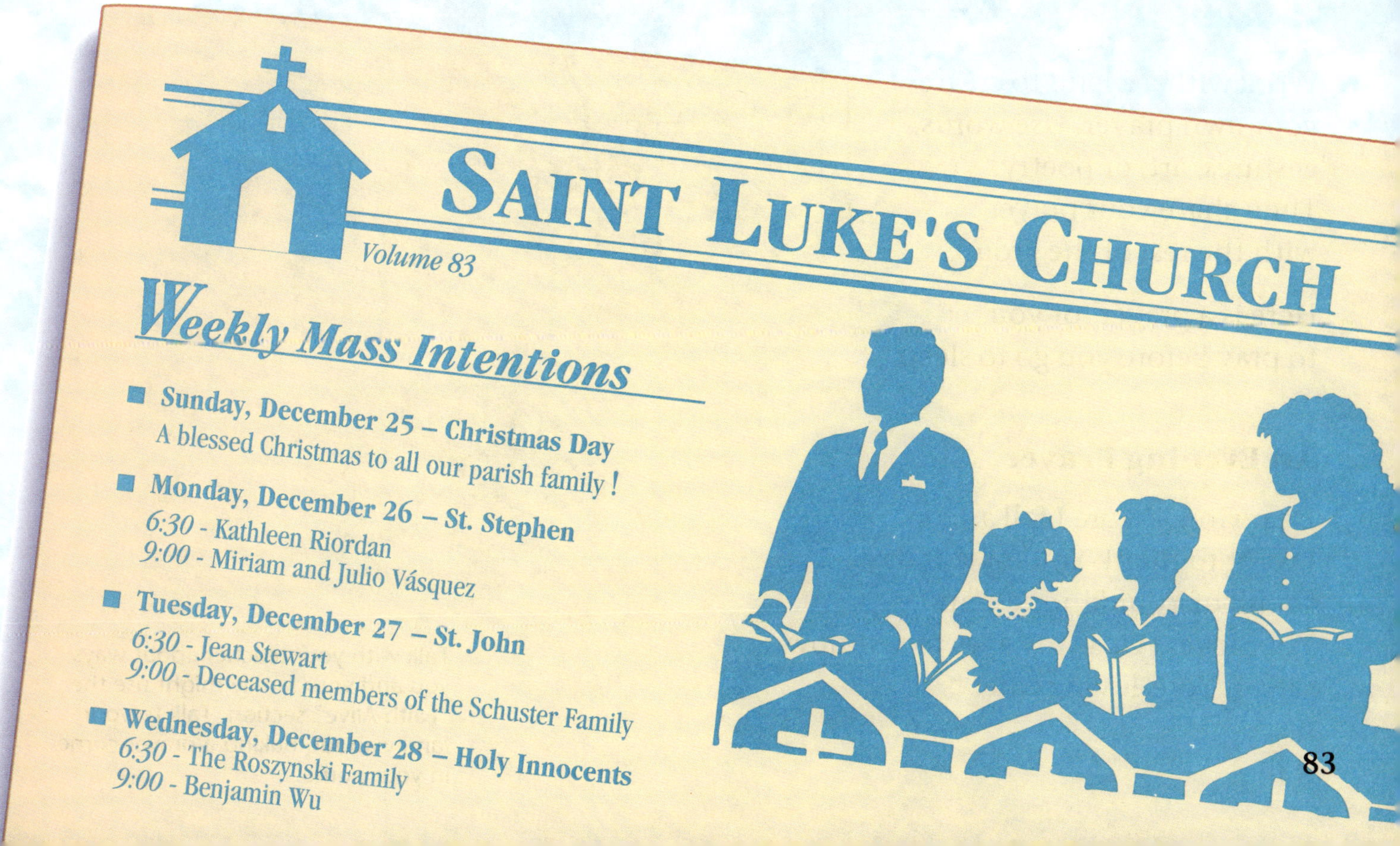

SAINT LUKE'S CHURCH

Volume 83

Weekly Mass Intentions

- **Sunday, December 25 – Christmas Day**
  A blessed Christmas to all our parish family!

- **Monday, December 26 – St. Stephen**
  6:30 - Kathleen Riordan
  9:00 - Miriam and Julio Vásquez

- **Tuesday, December 27 – St. John**
  6:30 - Jean Stewart
  9:00 - Deceased members of the Schuster Family

- **Wednesday, December 28 – Holy Innocents**
  6:30 - The Roszynski Family
  9:00 - Benjamin Wu

COMING TO FAITH

Name some reasons why we pray.

Talk over together how we can learn to pray better.

Tell what you know about the communion of saints.

What do you think about this part of our Catholic faith?

PRACTICING FAITH

Work with a friend to create your own prayer. Use words, gestures, art, or poetry. Then share your prayer with the rest of the group.

Here is a prayer for you to pray before you go to sleep.

✝ An Evening Prayer

Dear God, before I fall asleep
I want to thank You for this day,
so full of Your kindness and
Your love. I close my eyes to rest now,
safe in Your loving care.

Talk with your teacher about ways you and your family might use the "Faith Alive" section. Talk to your family about making a prayer corner in your home.

84

REVIEW • TEST

Circle the letter beside the correct answer.

1. Being named a saint by the Church is called
   a. celebration.
   b. liturgy.
   c. canonization.

2. On November 1 we celebrate the feast of
   a. All Saints.
   b. All Souls.
   c. the sacraments.

3. The patron saint of the whole Catholic Church is
   a. Saint John.
   b. Saint Peter.
   c. Saint Joseph.

4. November 2 is the feast of
   a. Thanksgiving.
   b. the Immaculate Conception.
   c. All Souls.

5. How can you try to be a saint?

_____

FAITH ALIVE AT HOME AND IN THE PARISH

In this lesson your child learned how we pray, both alone as individuals and together as a parish community. Share with your child the importance of prayer in your life. Discuss especially how to talk to Jesus both in quiet moments and in the midst of work. Developing the habit of personal prayer is essential for the spiritual growth of your child.

Your child also learned about the communion of saints. Help your child understand that all the members of the Church, both living and dead, are united by Baptism. Explain that since this bond is not broken, even by death, we can still help one another, especially through prayer.

Prayer Corner

If possible, set up a prayer corner in your home where your family can pray together. Display a picture of Jesus, Mary, or your favorite saint on a table covered with a cloth. Place a Bible nearby. If you wish, decorate the table according to the liturgical season of the Church or the season of the year.

Praying with Your Family

This week, try to set aside time when your family can pray together. You may want to pray together before and after meals, or you may want to say the Our Father and Hail Mary at a quiet time during the evening.

9   Our Parish Worships

Loving God, we
come to praise
and honor You.

Our Life

Look at the pictures.
These are some of the signs that
hearing impaired people sometimes
use to talk to one another.

Have you ever seen anyone use
sign language? Tell about it.

Try saying some of these words
with your hands. How does it
make you feel?

Are there other signs that have
special meaning for you?
Tell what these signs mean to you.

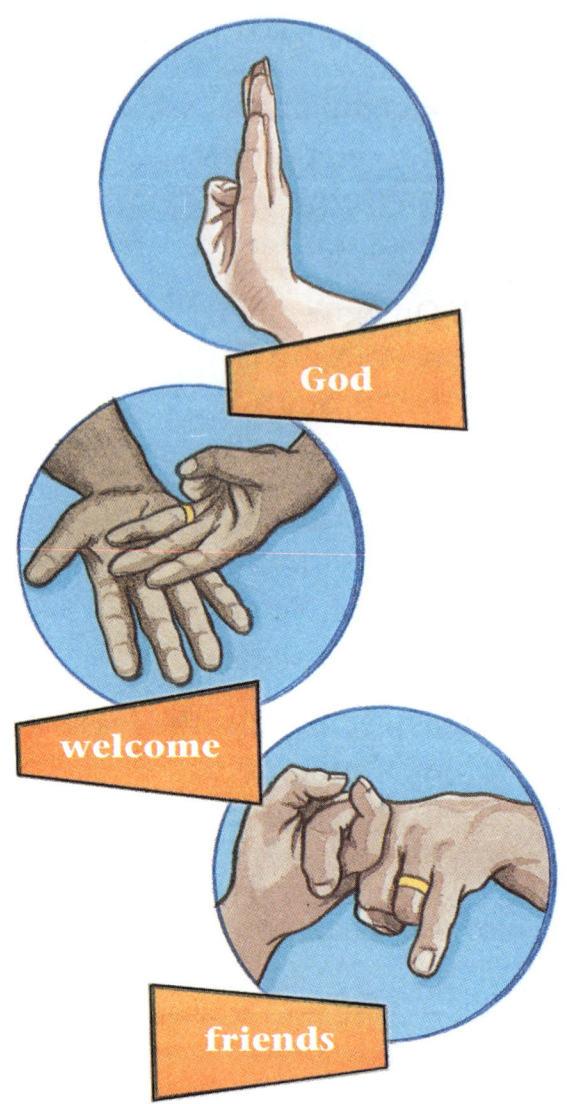

God

welcome

friends

Sharing Life

Why do we sometimes use signs
to say things to one another?

Are there times when signs
are even better than words
for saying what we mean?

What are some of the signs
that God uses to reach out to us?

With a partner, list some signs you use to show love for God or others.

_____

_____

_____

_____

Act out one sign for your group.

Now practice this sign with your partner.

When will you share this sign of love for God with your family and friends?

In this lesson we will explore seven special signs of love that Jesus has given us. They are the seven sacraments.

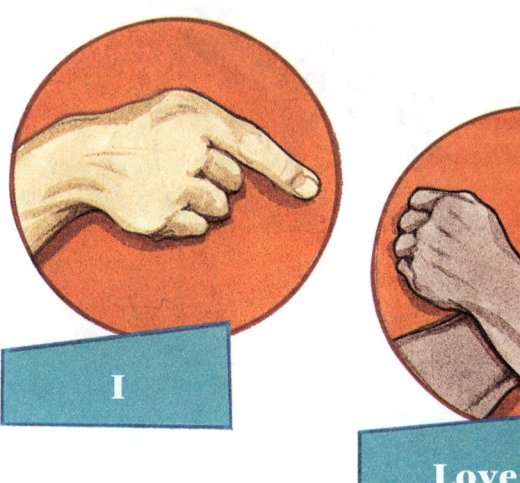

I

Love

You

God

☀ We Will Learn

- Our parish worships **God** through the seven sacraments.

- The sacraments of initiation welcome us into **the Church,** the body of Christ.

- The sacraments of healing and service help us to live **as Jesus'** followers.

OUR CATHOLIC FAITH

■ Thank You, God, for giving us signs of Your love.

■ What special signs of love do you receive? do you give?

The Seven Sacraments

The Catholic Church has seven powerful signs through which Jesus Christ shares God's life and love with us. We call these signs sacraments.

A sign is something we can see or hear, taste or touch. A sign tells us about something else that we cannot see. It points to something more important.

In the seven sacraments we use water, oil, bread and wine, words, and actions. Through these signs and by the power of the Holy Spirit, Jesus shares God's own life and love with us. We call God's life and love in us God's grace.

The sacraments bring us God's grace and help us to live as God's people. Joined together by the Holy Spirit, the Church gathers to celebrate the seven powerful signs that are the sacraments. We listen to God's word. We give praise and honor to God. Through the sacraments, Christ Himself gives us a share in God's grace. The praise and honor we give to God is called worship. The sacraments are our most powerful signs for worshiping God.

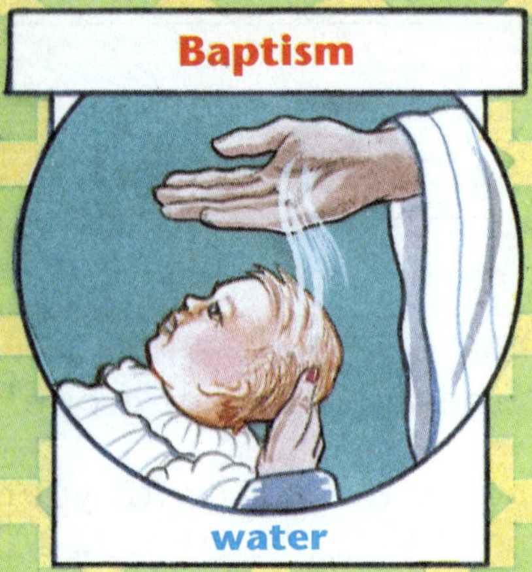

Baptism

water

Confirmation

holy oil

Eucharist

bread and wine

Reconciliation

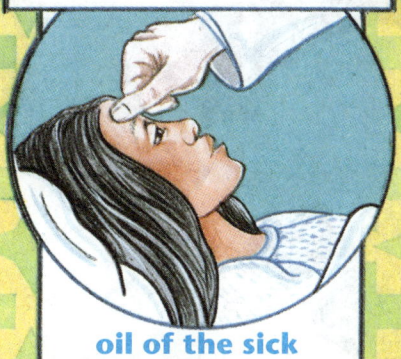

absolution

Anointing of the Sick

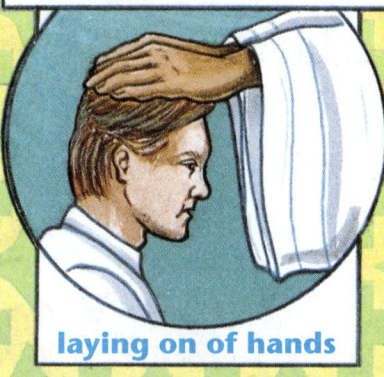

oil of the sick

Holy Orders

laying on of hands

Matrimony

marriage vows

FAITH WORD

Sacraments are powerful signs through which Jesus shares God's life and love with us in the community of the Church.

The sacraments of the Catholic Church are:		
Sacraments of Initiation	**Sacraments of Healing**	**Sacraments of Service**
Baptism	Reconciliation	Matrimony
Confirmation	Anointing of the Sick	Holy Orders
Eucharist		

Write the names of the sacraments you have celebrated so far in your life.

_____

_____

_____

_____

_____

- What is a sacrament?
- Make up a prayer to thank God for the gift of the sacraments.

OUR CATHOLIC FAITH

■ Jesus, help us to learn more about the celebration of the sacraments.

■ Why are the sacraments important to us?

Sacraments of Initiation

Three of the seven sacraments are called the sacraments of initiation, because through them we become members of the Church, the body of Christ. These sacraments are Baptism, Confirmation, and Eucharist.

Jesus invited everyone to belong to His community. He reached out in a special way to those who felt left out.

Today the Catholic Church does what Jesus did. We welcome all people and invite them to belong to Jesus' community, the Church. Baptism is the sacrament by which we are freed from sin, become children of God, and are welcomed as members of the Church.

Jesus knew it would not always be easy for His followers to live the Law of Love. So He gave them the Holy Spirit to be with them always.

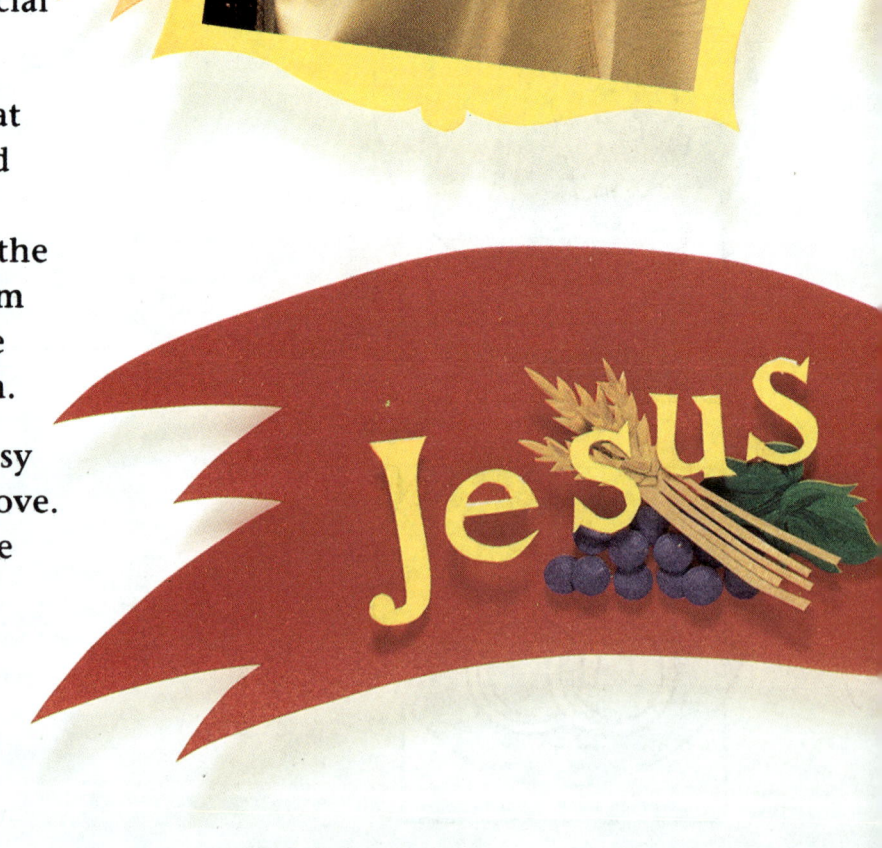

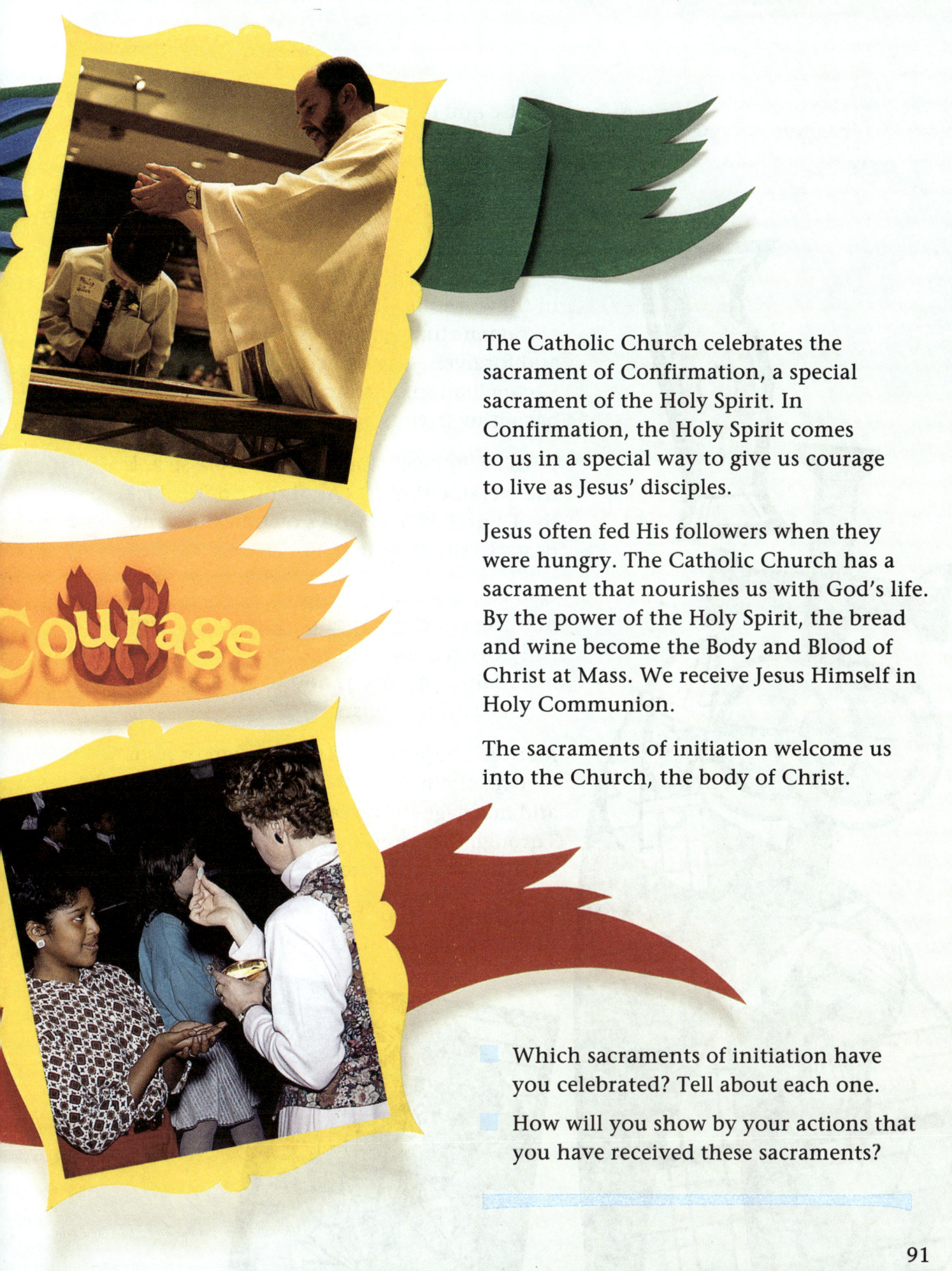

The Catholic Church celebrates the sacrament of Confirmation, a special sacrament of the Holy Spirit. In Confirmation, the Holy Spirit comes to us in a special way to give us courage to live as Jesus' disciples.

Jesus often fed His followers when they were hungry. The Catholic Church has a sacrament that nourishes us with God's life. By the power of the Holy Spirit, the bread and wine become the Body and Blood of Christ at Mass. We receive Jesus Himself in Holy Communion.

The sacraments of initiation welcome us into the Church, the body of Christ.

■ Which sacraments of initiation have you celebrated? Tell about each one.

■ How will you show by your actions that you have received these sacraments?

OuR
CATHOLIC
FAITH

■ Jesus, we praise and thank You for giving us the sacraments.

■ Name a sacrament you have not yet received. Tell what you know about it.

Sacraments of Healing and Service

In the Catholic Church we have a sacrament that celebrates God's love and forgiveness, the sacrament of Reconciliation. Reconciliation means becoming friends again.

Jesus often healed people who were sick. In the sacrament of the Anointing of the Sick, the Church brings God's own healing and peace to sick people.

God chooses certain people to be our special ministers in the Church. In the sacrament of Holy Orders, the Church chooses the men to be ordained ministers and to serve as bishops, priests, and deacons.

Married people have a special sign of Jesus' love for them. The Church blesses their love and marriage in the sacrament of Matrimony. Through their love, they serve each other and the whole Church.

The sacraments of healing and service help us to love and serve one another.

Signs of the Sacraments

Each sacrament has its own special sign. The signs of the sacraments are very important. We use bread and wine, water, oil, words, and even the sense of touch.

What is the special sign for each of these sacraments?

Baptism _____

Confirmation _____

Eucharist _____

Holy Orders _____

Anointing of the Sick _____

In two sacraments, words are used as special signs of God's love for us. Name these two sacraments. Tell what special sign is used in each of them.

_____

_____

Choose one sacrament. Make up a prayer to praise or thank God for the gift of that sacrament. Share your prayer.

Learn by heart **Faith Summary**

- We worship God through the seven sacraments.

- The sacraments of initiation welcome us into the Church community.

- The sacraments of healing and service help us to love and serve one another.

I ABSOLVE YOU

Share a Family Meal

COMING TO FAITH

Take turns telling about the sacraments you have taken part in so far.

Why do you think we celebrate the sacraments together?

Take Time to Pray

9   3

6

PRACTICING FAITH

Talk together about ways you can be a "living sacrament"—a sign of God's love for others.

Make up your own symbol for what you will do. Draw it on the poster and explain it.

Take turns sharing your posters. Then close by praying together, "Glory to the Father . . . ."

THANK GOD FOR CREATION

Talk with your teacher about ways you and your family might use the "Faith Alive" section. Work with your family on the Looking for Signs of Love activity.

94

REVIEW · TEST

Fill in the missing word or words.

1. Powerful signs through which Jesus shares God's life with us are called

_____.

2. The sacraments of initiation are _____,

_____ and _____.

3. The sacraments of healing are _____

and _____.

4. The sacraments of service are _____

and _____.

5. Tell about one sacrament you have received and what it means to you.

_____

_____

_____

FAITH ALIVE — AT HOME AND IN THE PARISH

In this lesson your child learned that the sacraments are signs through which Jesus, by the power of the Holy Spirit, shares God's life and love with us. Ask your child to tell you about each sacrament. Then talk about his or her own Baptism and any other sacraments celebrated.

Looking for Signs of Love

Talk with your family about the various signs through which you show your love for one another. Include words ("I forgive you"), gestures (hugs, kisses), and loving actions (keeping promises, caring for a sick family member, preparing a favorite dessert). Invite your family to spend a day or two observing and recording signs of love within the family. Share your findings. As much as possible, relate them to the sacraments as special signs of God's love for us.

Blessing One Another

Sharing a blessing is a sign of our faith and trust in God's loving care. Take a few minutes to bless your child at bedtime. Place your hands on your child's head and pray, "May the Lord Jesus bless you and keep you safe now and forever." If you wish, invite your child to bless you, too.

Dear God,
forgive us
as we forgive
others.

OUR LIFE

One day, Jesus told a story to teach about God's great forgiveness. There was a rich man who had two sons. One of them wanted his share of his father's money so he could go and see the world. After he received it, he got in with a bad crowd and lost all his money.

One day the son woke up poor, dirty, and hungry. He said to himself, "I will go back home to my father and say, 'Father, I have sinned against God and you. I am no longer fit to be called your son. Treat me as one of your hired hands.'"

One day the father saw his son returning home. He rushed out and hugged his son in welcome. Then he shouted to his servants, "Let us have a wonderful feast to celebrate! My son has come home!"
From Luke 15:11–32

What does this story tell us about God's forgiveness?

SHARING LIFE

Quietly think of something you have done for which you need to be forgiven.

What do you think God will say to you when you say you are sorry?

Share your thoughts with a friend.

Imagine you are a TV news reporter covering the celebration to welcome the son home. Your task is to interview either the son or his father.

Whom will you interview?

_____

What question will you ask him?

_____

_____

What do you think his answer will be?

_____

_____

Share your interview with your group.

In this lesson we will learn more about the way God welcomes us and forgives us in the sacrament of Reconciliation.

☀ We Will Learn

- We prepare for Reconciliation by examining our conscience.

- We can celebrate the sacrament of Reconciliation alone or with others.

- Jesus wants us to forgive others.

God, You are always ready to forgive us.

What should we do when we need to be forgiven?

We Prepare for Reconciliation

We are Jesus' community, the Church. We try to live as Jesus' disciples. But sometimes we do not love God and others as Jesus wants us to love them.

We are selfish or unfair. We do things that we know are wrong. We sin.

Sin is freely choosing to do what we know is wrong. We disobey God's law on purpose.

Some sins are so serious that by doing them we turn away completely from God's love. We call them mortal sins. Sin is mortal when:

- what we do is very seriously wrong;
- we know that it is wrong and that God forbids it;
- we freely choose to do it.

Less serious sins are called venial sins. We hurt others and ourselves, but we do not turn away completely from God's love. Venial sins make us less loving members of Jesus' community.

God is like the forgiving father in the story. God wants us to be sorry for our sins and waits to forgive us.

When we are truly sorry for our sins, God always forgives us. In the Catholic Church we celebrate God's forgiveness in the sacrament of Reconciliation, or Penance. We celebrate Reconciliation with the priest either by ourselves or with others.

We get ready to celebrate Reconciliation by asking ourselves how well we have loved God, others, and ourselves. We also think about what our parents and the Church teach us about what is right and wrong. We call this our examination of conscience. Our conscience lets us know when something we have done is right or wrong. Our parents and the Church help us to know right from wrong. The Holy Spirit helps us to examine our conscience.

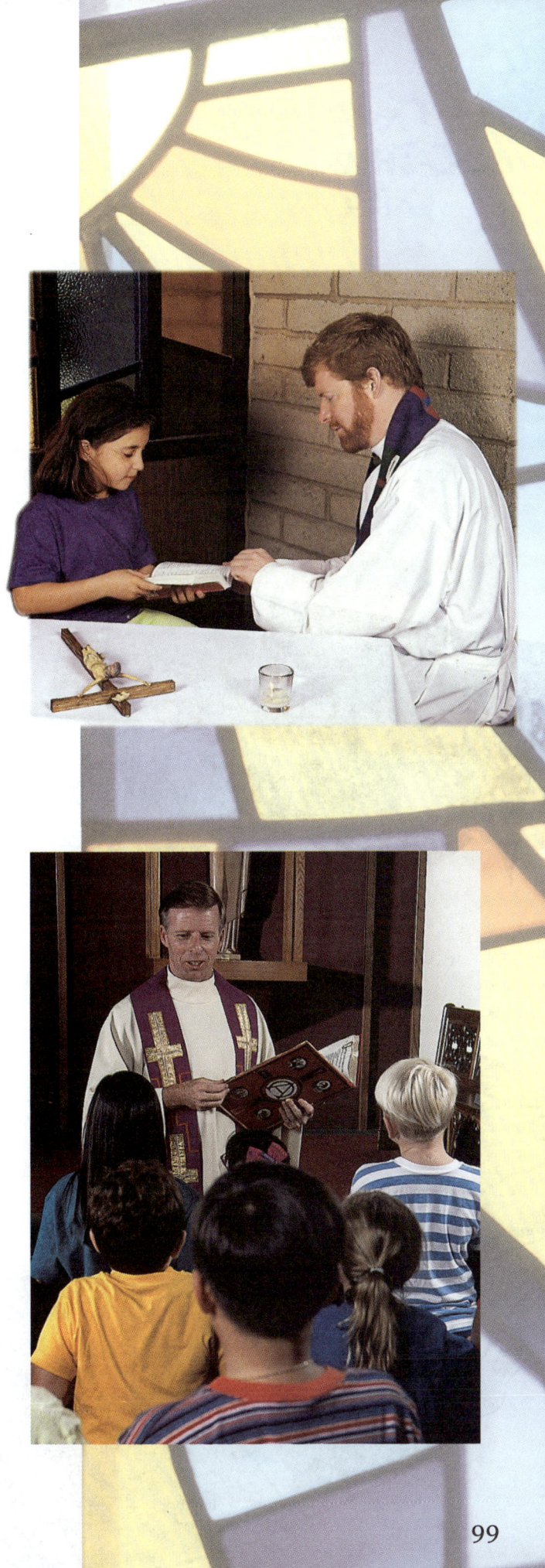

- Tell how you know something is a sin.
- Tell how you can prepare to celebrate the sacrament of Reconciliation.

OUR CATHOLIC FAITH

- We praise You, O God, for the gift of Your mercy and love.

- How do you give and receive forgiveness?

We Celebrate Reconciliation

These are two ways we can celebrate the sacrament of Reconciliation, or Penance:

- by ourselves, with the priest;

- with the priest and others in our parish family.

In the Individual Rite of Reconciliation, we meet the priest in a special place called the reconciliation room. We can sit and talk to him face-to-face, or we can kneel behind a screen and tell our sins without the priest knowing who we are. We call this confession.

In the Communal Rite of Reconciliation, we come together with the priest and people from our parish. We sing hymns and listen to readings from the Bible. Then we go one by one to the priest to confess our sins.

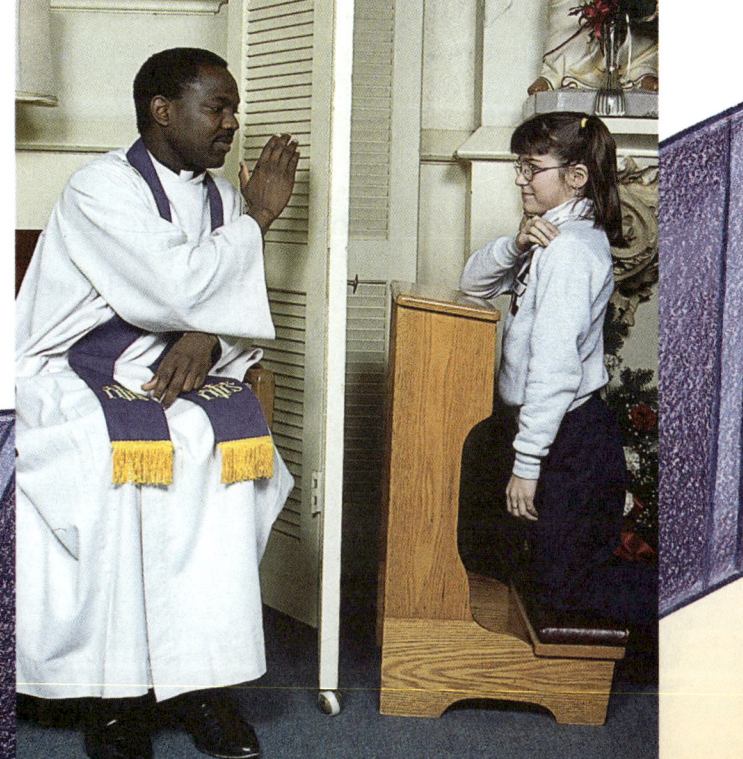

Remember, the priest will never tell anyone what we say to him in confession. The priest listens to our sins and gives us advice about ways to be better disciples of Jesus.

Then the priest asks us to say a prayer or do something to make up for our sins. This is called a penance. We say an Act of Contrition to show that we are sorry for our sins. We promise to try harder to avoid sin and to do good.

Next, we receive absolution. Absolution means being freed from our sins. The priest forgives us in God's name and in the name of the Church. He places his hand over our head and says, "Through the ministry of the Church may God give you pardon and peace, and I absolve you from your sins in the name of the Father, and of the Son,✝ and of the Holy Spirit."

Confession is telling our sins to the priest in the sacrament of Reconciliation.

Celebrating Reconciliation
1. We examine our conscience.
2. We confess our sins to the priest.
3. The priest gives us a penance.
4. We say an Act of Contrition.
5. We receive absolution.
6. We thank God and do our penance.

Explain two ways we can celebrate the sacrament of Reconciliation.

When will you celebrate Reconciliation?

101

OUR CATHOLIC FAITH

■ Pray the Our Father together.

■ Does God want us to forgive others? Why?

People of Forgiveness and Peace

After celebrating the wonderful and healing sacrament of Reconciliation, we thank God. We know our sins are forgiven through the power of the Holy Spirit. The Holy Spirit will give us the help we need to love God, to love others, and to love ourselves.

Jesus wants us to forgive others as God has forgiven us. In the Our Father, He taught us to pray, "Forgive us our trespasses, as we forgive those who trespass against us."

Reconciliation also means making peace. We can be peacemakers by trying to make up when we have had a fight. We can pray for peace in our world. The sacrament of Reconciliation helps us to be peacemakers.

Our whole parish can become a community of forgiveness and peace. We help this to happen when we celebrate the sacrament of Reconciliation often.

The Reconciliation Room

Not too long ago, most Catholics celebrated the sacrament of Reconciliation in a small place called the confessional box. The priest sat inside the box between two screens. A person who wanted to confess entered the box and knelt beside one of the screens. The priest then heard the person's confession through the screen.

Today in most churches, the place of confession of sins has changed. Most Catholics now meet with the priest in the reconciliation room. There, we have a choice. We can confess our sins through a screen or face-to-face with the priest.

Look at the pictures. Where would you like to celebrate Reconciliation?

Will you ask God to help you prepare to receive this wonderful sacrament of God's love and forgiveness?

Learn by heart Faith Summary

- We prepare for Reconciliation by examining our conscience.

- We celebrate Reconciliation with the priest either by ourselves or with others from the parish community.

- Reconciliation helps us to forgive others.

103

Coming To Faith

Read each story below. Tell what each person should do, and why.

Martha is in the mall. She sees a watch she wants but can't afford. "I could take it. No one will see," she thinks.

Craig's mother says, "You can't watch TV unless your homework is done." Craig has math homework to do.

How does the sacrament of Reconciliation help us live as disciples of Jesus?

Practicing Faith

Act out the story of the forgiving father. Then sing together:
(to the tune of "Down by the Station")

♫ Every day the father waited
  for his son's returning.
Every day he waited, waited,
  and his heart was yearning.
"Oh my child, come back to me.
  I always will forgive.
Oh my child, come back to me
  and you will surely live!"♫

Is there someone whose forgiveness you need? What will you do?

Is there someone you need to forgive? What will you do?

Now pray the Our Father together. Think about its words of forgiveness.

Talk with your teacher about ways you and your family might use the "Faith Alive" section. Tell someone in your family the steps for celebrating Reconciliation. Pray the Forgiveness Prayer with your teacher and friends.

REVIEW • TEST

Circle the letter beside the correct answer.

1. When we freely choose to do things we know are wrong, we

    a. make a mistake.   **b.** sin.   **c.** avoid temptation.

2. A sin that completely separates us from God is called

    a. mortal sin.   **b.** original sin.   **c.** venial sin.

3. A prayer that tells God we are sorry is the

    a. Apostles' Creed.   **b.** Our Father.   **c.** Act of Contrition.

4. Telling our sins to the priest is called

    a. absolution.   **b.** confession.   **c.** penance.

5. How can we celebrate God's forgiveness in the Church?

_____

_____

_____

FAITH ALIVE AT HOME AND IN THE PARISH

This week your child has learned more about the ways to celebrate the sacrament of Reconciliation, or Penance. Talk to your child about the following two ways of celebrating this sacrament.

In the Individual Rite, we each meet with the priest in the reconciliation room. We can sit and talk to him face-to-face, or we can kneel behind a screen.

In the Communal Rite, together with the priest and people from our parish, we pray to the Holy Spirit and thank God for the gift of forgiveness. We sing hymns and listen to readings from Scripture. We each go to the priest to confess our sins and receive absolution.

Forgiveness Story

At times family members need to ask forgiveness of one another. Gather with your family and have someone read aloud the story of the forgiving father on page 96. Then allow quiet time for each person to think about something for which he or she is sorry. Have each person say, "If I have done anything to hurt you, I am sorry." Everyone responds, "I forgive you."

† Forgiveness Prayer

Pray this forgiveness prayer together.

Merciful God, hear our prayer. Forgive the sins of those who confess to You. Give us Your peace. We ask this through Jesus Christ. Amen.

O God, we come
before You
with joy and
thanksgiving.

Our Life

At a special meal on the night before
He died, Jesus took bread, broke it,
and gave it to His disciples, saying,
"Take and eat this. This is My Body."

Then Jesus took a cup of wine and gave
thanks to God. Jesus handed the cup
to His friends, saying, "Drink this, all
of you. This is My Blood poured out
for many for the forgiveness of sin."
From Matthew 26:26–28

After this, Jesus told His disciples,
"Do this in memory of Me." Now Jesus
would be with His friends forever in
the Eucharist.

What is Jesus saying to His disciples
in this story?

What gift do you bring to
Jesus at Mass?

Sharing Life

Imagine you had been at the
Last Supper. What do you
think Jesus meant by
"Do this in memory of Me"?

What do you think is the most
special way Jesus is present
with us?

As Catholics, we believe that Jesus is with us in a special way at Mass. With your group, share ways you can get ready to celebrate with Jesus at Mass. Write some ideas here.

_____

_____

_____

_____

Why do you think it is important to prepare for our celebration of the Mass?

In this lesson we will explore how each of us helps to make the Mass a great celebration.

We Will Learn

- Our parish celebrates the Eucharist as a community.

- Many people help us to celebrate well.

- Each of us has a part to play in the celebration of the Mass.

107

■ We thank You, Jesus, for really being with us in the Eucharist.

■ Why do you think the Mass is our greatest celebration?

Our Parish Celebrates the Eucharist

Each week our parish community assembles for the most important celebration we share, the Mass. The Mass is our greatest prayer of praise and thanks to God. The Mass is our celebration of the Eucharist. At Mass, we remember what Jesus did at the Last Supper.

The Mass is both a meal and a sacrifice. The Mass is a meal at which Jesus gives us the gift of Himself to be our food. The Mass is also a sacrifice. At Mass we share in Jesus' gift of Himself to God. We remember and celebrate Jesus' life, death, and resurrection. Jesus died to save us from sin and bring us new life.

Jesus rose from the dead on Easter Sunday and is with us always. Every time we join in the celebration of the Mass, it is like celebrating Easter.

The **Mass** is our celebration of Jesus' special meal and sacrifice.

Each of us has a part to play in the celebration of the Mass. It is very important that we be present. The Catholic Church makes it a serious responsibility for its members to take part in the Mass each week on Sunday, or Saturday evening, and on holy days of obligation.

It is not always easy for us to get to Mass. Some people must work or travel when Mass is being celebrated. But we are to do all we possibly can to get to Mass each week. This is a serious responsibility of our Catholic faith.

If no one in our family goes to Mass, we should try to go by ourselves or with a friend. We should pray that our whole family will come to know that the Mass is our best way of worshiping God together.

■ What do we remember and celebrate at Mass?

■ How will you try to join in the celebration of Mass each Sunday?

109

OUR CATHOLIC FAITH

- Loving God, we praise and thank You for the gift of Jesus at Mass.

- What things do you like to do at Mass?

Everyone Helps to Celebrate

Everyone present helps in the celebration of Mass. We do this by praying together and actively taking part in the celebration.

Many people in our parish have special roles in our great celebration of Mass. The lectors read to us from the Bible. There is usually one reading from the Old Testament. The other readings are always taken from the New Testament. The priest or deacon reads from one of the gospels.

The eucharistic ministers help the priest and deacon to give us Holy Communion. Sometimes they bring Communion to those who cannot come to Mass.

Altar servers light the altar candles. They make sure that the water and wine are ready for the celebration. During the Mass they help, or serve, the priest.

The ushers welcome us and help us to find seats. They collect our donations during Mass. The musicians and the choir choose songs for us to sing. Our choir leads us in praying to God through song.

All of these people help us to take part in the Mass. We must do our best to join in the celebration.

Name those who help at Mass in your parish. Draw one person who helps at Mass.

- Take time to thank God for all those who help to make the celebration of the Mass so wonderful.

- How will you join in the celebration of the Mass?

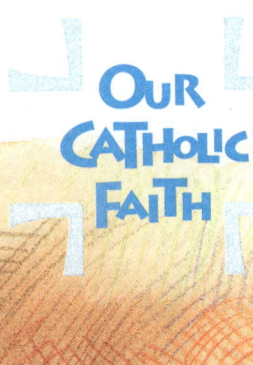

OUR CATHOLIC FAITH

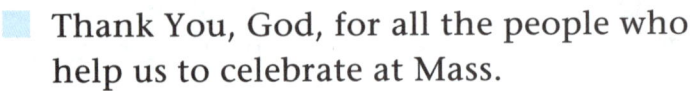

■ Thank You, God, for all the people who help us to celebrate at Mass.

■ Why must we do our best to join in the celebration of Mass?

How We Take Part

Everyone in our parish family has a part to play in our celebration of the Eucharist. These are some ways we help make the Mass a great celebration:

- We join in the singing.

- We join in prayer with the rest of the assembly.

- We listen to the Scripture readings and to the homily given by the priest or deacon.

- We offer to God all the good things we have done during the past week.

- We give the sign of peace to others.

- We pray quietly to Jesus after receiving Holy Communion.

- We decide how we will bring the peace and love of Jesus to others in the coming week.

Serving at the Altar

Altar servers have an important role at Mass. Here are some ways these boys and girls help our parish family celebrate together.

- Altar servers lead the procession at the beginning of Mass. They may carry lighted candles, a large cross, and even incense when it is used at Mass.

- Altar servers help the priest receive and prepare our gifts of bread and wine.

Can you name other ways they help the priest during Mass?

It is a wonderful privilege to serve at the altar and to help our parish family worship God together.

Do you think you would like to be an altar server? Tell why or why not.

Learn by heart **Faith Summary**

- The Mass is both a meal and a sacrifice.

- The Mass is our greatest prayer of praise and thanks to God.

- Catholics must take part in the Mass each Sunday or Saturday evening.

COMING TO FAITH

How do you feel knowing that Jesus is with us when we celebrate Mass?

Tell what you can do at your age to help your parish get ready for Mass this week.

What can you do when you get older?

Share together why the Mass is so important to Catholics.

JESUS INVITES US TO CELEBRATE!

PRACTICING FAITH

Jesus invites us to celebrate together as a parish community at Mass.

Make a group poster or banner of Jesus' invitation and decorate it with pictures or symbols of what we do together at Mass.

Make a plan to attend Mass with your group this week and display your banner invitation at one of the church doors.

Talk with your teacher about ways you and your family might use the "Faith Alive" section. Work with your family on preparing a special Sunday celebration.

REVIEW ■ TEST

Complete the sentences.

1. The Mass is our celebration of Jesus' special meal and _____.

2. Catholics have a serious responsibility to take part in the Mass on

_____.

3. Those who help the priest during Mass are called altar _____.

4. Those who read to us at Mass are called _____.

5. What special thing would you like to do to take part in the Mass?

_____

_____

_____

FAITH ALIVE AT HOME AND IN THE PARISH

In this lesson your child learned the importance of taking part in the parish celebration of the Eucharist. Your own enthusiasm for taking part in the Mass each week can help your child to be enthusiastic as well. Keeping the Sabbath holy by taking part in the celebration of Mass is a central aspect of our Catholic identity and one of the laws of the Church. It is your responsibility to help your child develop this lifelong habit.

Sunday Celebration

Plan a Sunday celebration with your family. You may want to worship together at Mass and then share a family meal, outing, or at-home activity.

At an appropriate time, talk about the joy in knowing that Jesus is with us in our home and with us in a special way when we celebrate Mass with our parish family.

Our Gifts to God

One way we participate in the Mass is by offering God all the good things we have done during the past week. With your family, make a list of at least one good thing each member has done. If you wish, title the list "Our Gifts to God" and have your child make a decorative border for the page. Before going to Mass, read the list aloud. Remind your family to think about the good things they have done as the gifts of bread and wine are brought to the altar.

Jesus, Lamb of God, grant us peace.

Our Life

Livia and her brother were out of breath. "Hurry, Marcus," Livia gasped. "The community is coming to our house for the Eucharist. And the apostle will be here!"

They hurried into the room where their mother had prepared a table with bread and wine. Soon their Christian friends began arriving—many bringing food and money to share with those in need.

Everyone greeted one another warmly with signs of peace and love. They sang psalms and listened carefully as the apostle spoke about Jesus—what He had said and done, and how He wanted His followers to live. Then the apostle blessed and broke the bread. He blessed the wine, too, as Jesus had done. And everyone received the Body and Blood of Christ with great joy. Livia loved being a part of her Christian gathering.

What do you like best about this early Christian celebration of the Eucharist?

What do you like best about today's celebration in your parish?

Sharing Life

What is the same now as it was then?

What is different?

The Mass today is basically the same as the early Church's celebration of the Eucharist. What we do together at Mass links us to all those who have celebrated the Eucharist before us.

On each link, write one thing we do at Mass today that the Church community has always done. Explain why we do these things at every Mass.

In this lesson we will learn more about our great celebration of the Mass.

We Will Learn

- God speaks to us in the Liturgy of the Word.

- In the Liturgy of the Eucharist, our gifts of bread and wine become the Body and Blood of Christ.

- When we leave Mass, we are to love and serve others.

■ Thank You, Jesus, for giving us the gift of Yourself at Mass.

■ Tell your favorite Bible story.

Introductory Rites

As Mass begins, we gather and prepare to become a worshiping community. The priest welcomes the assembled people of our parish. Together we make the sign of the cross and begin our celebration. We remember that we are a community offering our gifts to God the Father, through the Son, and by the power of the Holy Spirit.

Then we remember that we need God's mercy. We tell God we are sorry for our sins and ask God to forgive us.

Together we say the prayer of praise that begins "Glory to God in the highest." In this prayer we praise God and ask God's forgiveness and blessings.

Liturgy of the Word

Now we begin the part of the Mass called the Liturgy of the Word. We hear two readings from Scripture. Then the priest or deacon reads the gospel. We stand to show our respect for the good news of Jesus.

Then the priest or deacon gives a homily to help us apply the Scripture readings to our lives. After this we think and pray about God's word.

After the homily we stand to say the creed, a summary of our Catholic faith from the early Church.

Then we pray together for God's blessings on ourselves and on all people. This is called the Prayer of the Faithful. This prayer ends the Liturgy of the Word.

Write a prayer for the Prayer of the Faithful.

_____

_____

_____

_____

_____

Why should we listen carefully to God's word at Mass?

For whom will you pray at Mass this week?

OUR CATHOLIC FAITH

■ God, Your word helps us to live as Your people.

■ Why do you want to receive Jesus in Holy Communion?

Liturgy of the Eucharist

We now begin the part of the Mass called the Liturgy of the Eucharist. We present our gifts of bread and wine and bring them to the altar. The priest asks God to accept and bless our gifts. With our gifts, we offer our whole lives to God. Then we praise and thank God with the prayer that begins "Holy, holy, holy Lord."

Now begins the Eucharistic Prayer. If you listen and watch, you will see the priest say and do what Jesus said and did at the Last Supper.

The priest takes the bread and says, "Take this, all of you, and eat it: this is my body which will be given up for you." Then he takes the cup of wine and says, "Take this, all of you, and drink from it: this is the cup of my blood. Do this in memory of me."

We know that through the words and actions of the priest and the power of the Holy Spirit, the bread and wine become the Body and Blood of Christ.

We join with the priest and the whole Church in offering everything to God our Father through Jesus. At the end of the Eucharistic Prayer, we say or sing "Amen."

We begin the Communion of the Mass by praying or singing together the Our Father. The priest prays that Jesus Christ will give us the gift of His peace. We greet one another with a sign of Christ's peace. Then the priest takes the Host and breaks it while we say or sing the Lamb of God prayer.

Amen means "Yes, I believe."

If we are ready, we may receive Jesus' Body and Blood in Holy Communion. We hear the words, "The body of Christ." We answer, "Amen."

The Host is placed in our hands or on our tongues. Sometimes we also can drink from the chalice. After Holy Communion there is a quiet time for each of us to thank God for the gift of Jesus. This is a special time to tell Jesus what is in our hearts.

■ In what special way is Jesus with us in the Liturgy of the Eucharist?

■ What will you say to Jesus in the quiet time after Communion?

121

OUR CATHOLIC FAITH

■ Jesus, we believe You are really present in Holy Communion.

■ How can you thank Jesus for coming to you in Holy Communion?

Go in Peace

At the end of our Mass celebration, the priest blesses us. As he does so, we make the sign of the cross. Then the priest or deacon tells us to "go in peace to love and serve the Lord."

We answer, "Thanks be to God."

We know that this Mass is over and that it is time for us to leave. But the Mass never really ends. We live the Mass when we try to love and serve one another as disciples of Jesus.

With the help of the Holy Spirit, we will bring Jesus' peace to our families and friends. We will be fair to everyone and try to love and serve others. We will remember that Jesus is with us now and always.

Preparing the Wine at Mass

During the preparation of the gifts, the priest prepares the gifts of wine and water. He pours some wine into the chalice. Then he adds a little water to that wine.

As the priest pours the wine and the water, he quietly prays, "By the mystery of this water and wine may we come to share in the divinity of Christ, who humbled himself to share in our humanity."

The words and actions of the priest remind us that Jesus is true God and true Man. Jesus is God and one of us. He is both divine and human. By becoming one of us, Jesus made it possible for us to share in God's own life and love.

When you see the priest pouring the wine and water, will you try to remember what the words and the actions mean?

Learn by heart **Faith Summary**

- We listen to the Scripture readings in the Liturgy of the Word.

- In the Liturgy of the Eucharist, the gifts of bread or wine become the Body and Blood of Christ.

- We live the Mass by loving and serving God and other people.

COMING TO FAITH

The two main parts of the Mass are the

Liturgy of the _____ and the

Liturgy of the _____.

Make a list of ways third graders can "go in peace to love and serve the Lord."

PRACTICING FAITH

Write your ideas, then share them with one another.

What will you do this week to take part in the Mass?

_____

_____

Who can help you?

_____

_____

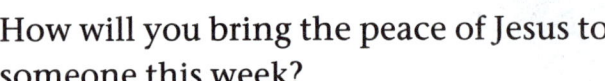

How will you bring the peace of Jesus to someone this week?

_____

_____

Talk with your teacher about ways you and your family might use the "Faith Alive" section. With your family, write a prayer to thank Jesus for the gift of Himself in Holy Communion.

REVIEW · TEST

Circle the letter beside the correct answer.

1. A prayer of praise we say at the beginning of Mass is

    a. "Holy, holy, holy Lord."

    b. "Glory to God in the highest."

    c. the Creed.

2. We pray for the needs of all people in

    a. the Our Father.

    b. the Scripture readings.

    c. the Prayer of the Faithful.

3. The bread and wine become the Body and Blood of Christ during the

    a. Eucharistic Prayer.

    b. Introductory Rites.

    c. Liturgy of the Word.

4. When we receive Jesus in Holy Communion, we say

    a. "Glory to God."

    b. "Lamb of God."

    c. "Amen."

5. How can you help others know that Jesus is with us at Mass?

FAITH ALIVE AT HOME AND IN THE PARISH

In this lesson your child learned more about the two major parts of the Mass: the Liturgy of the Word and the Liturgy of the Eucharist. Ask your child to tell you what he or she knows about each part of the Mass.

Our Family's Creed

During the Liturgy of the Word, we profess our faith as Catholics by praying the creed. Invite your family to share what the creed means to them. (If possible, use a parish missalette or a copy of the creed as reference.) Then make up a simple, brief creed that your family might benefit from praying together. Encourage family members to let their faith statements flow from the heart.

Example: We believe that God made us and loves us always. We believe that Jesus is God's Son and our Savior. We believe that the Holy Spirit helps us to live as Jesus' disciples. We believe that one day we will be with God forever in heaven. Amen.

✝ Thank You Prayer

Ask your family to share their feelings about the gift of Jesus in Holy Communion. Then compose a family prayer to thank Jesus for being really present in Holy Communion. Pray your family prayer after Mass this weekend.

13 | Advent

O come,
O come,
Emmanuel!

OUR LIFE

Here is a poem about waiting.
Finish it with your own words.

For _____ to begin,

For my favorite _____ to win,

For the _____ to bake,
It's very, very hard to wait.

For my _____ to come,

For _____ to be done,

I hope _____ isn't late.
It's very, very hard to wait!

Share your finished poem.

What are you waiting or hoping for?

SHARING LIFE

What do you think our Church is
waiting and hoping for?

126

With your group, make a list of things families could do while they wait and prepare for the celebration of Jesus' birth at Christmas.

From the list, choose several things your family might enjoy doing. Then make a card to invite them to do these things during Advent.

Here is a suggestion for making your card.

- Fold a large sheet of paper in half.

- On the front cover, write a message such as "O come, O come, Emmanuel." Decorate the cover.

- On the inside, write your own invitation or copy these words.

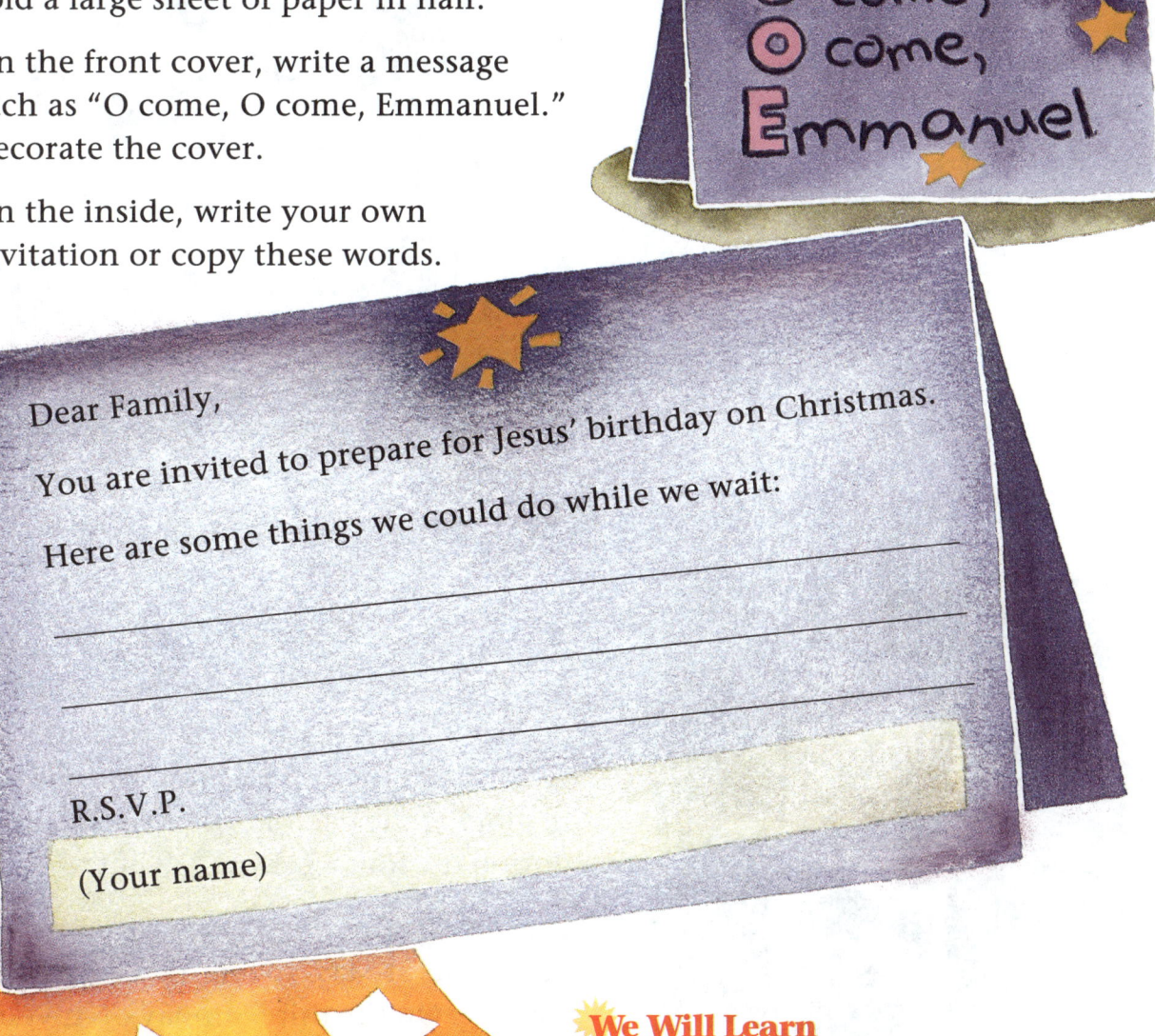

Dear Family,

You are invited to prepare for Jesus' birthday on Christmas.

Here are some things we could do while we wait:

_____

_____

_____

_____

R.S.V.P.

(Your name)

We Will Learn

- Jesus came to be our Savior.

- During Advent we prepare to celebrate Jesus' birth and wait for Him to come again in glory.

Our Catholic Faith

We Prepare to Welcome Jesus

Each year the Church celebrates a special time of waiting in the liturgical year. We call it the season of Advent.

Advent reminds us of the many hundreds of years God's people waited for God's promise of a Savior. During these long years of waiting, God spoke to the people through the prophets. The prophets told them to prepare for the Savior who was to come. The people were to:

• pray and worship God;

• care for the poor;

• be God's peacemakers;

• be just and fair to everyone.

As Catholics we believe that Jesus came to be our Savior. Each year we prepare ourselves to celebrate His birth, and we get ready as we wait for Him to come again in glory at the end of time. We do this during the four weeks of Advent.

During Advent, the priest wears purple vestments at Mass to remind us that we are waiting. On the third Sunday of Advent he sometimes wears rose or pink instead. This is a sign of the joy we feel because Christmas is near.

One way we can get ready to celebrate Jesus' coming is by making an Advent Calendar. The calendar should have four large pages, one for each week of Advent.

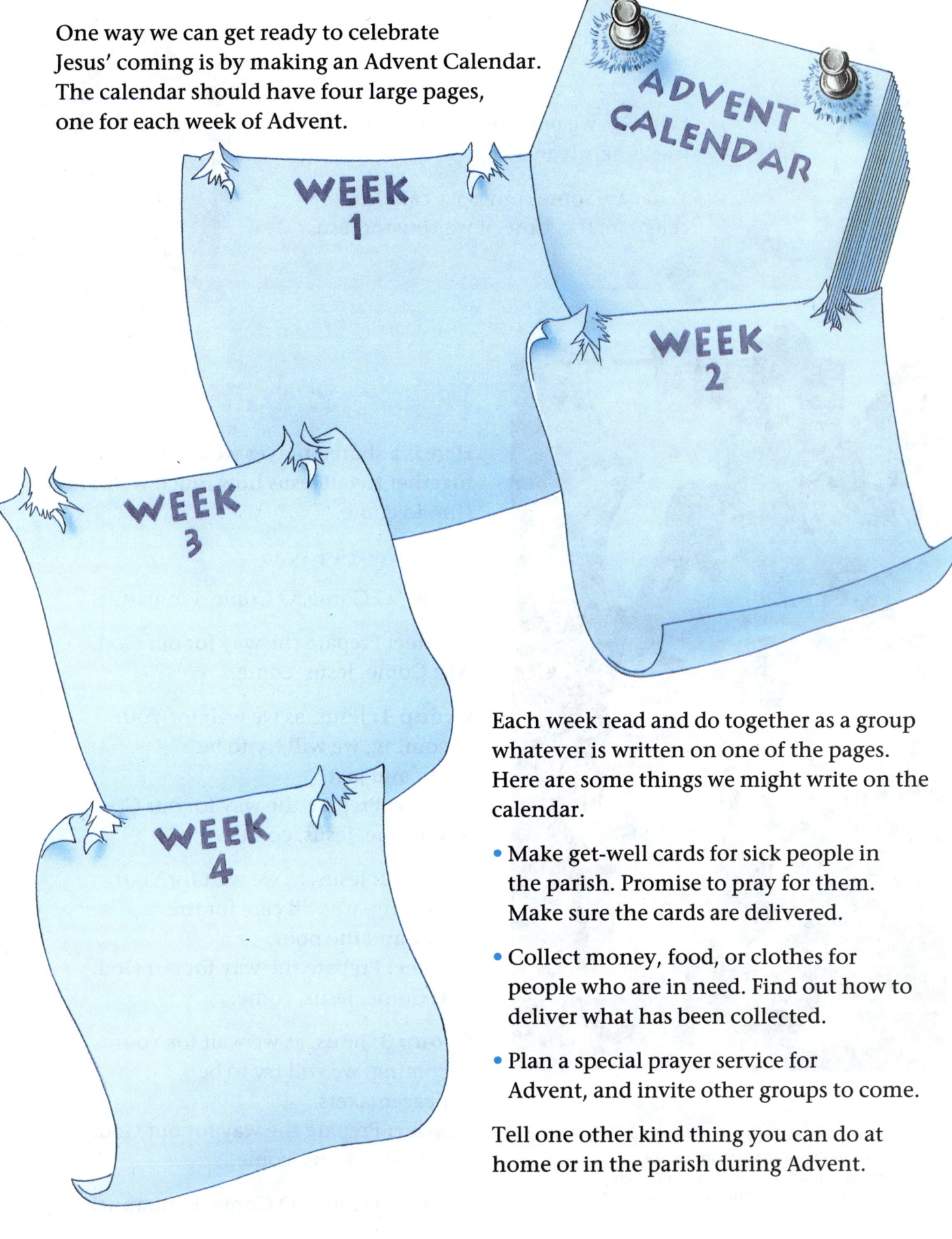

Each week read and do together as a group whatever is written on one of the pages. Here are some things we might write on the calendar.

- Make get-well cards for sick people in the parish. Promise to pray for them. Make sure the cards are delivered.

- Collect money, food, or clothes for people who are in need. Find out how to deliver what has been collected.

- Plan a special prayer service for Advent, and invite other groups to come.

Tell one other kind thing you can do at home or in the parish during Advent.

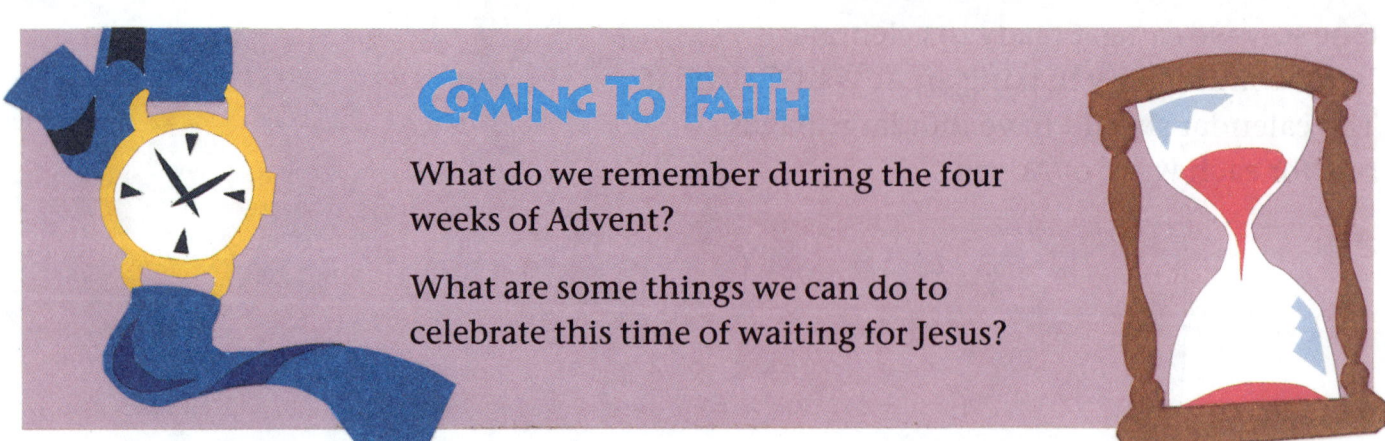

COMING TO FAITH

What do we remember during the four weeks of Advent?

What are some things we can do to celebrate this time of waiting for Jesus?

Talk with your teacher about ways you and your family can use the "Faith Alive" section. During Advent, pray Psalm 100 with your family.

PRACTICING FAITH

Here is a shared prayer we can say together to tell Jesus how much we want Him to come.

An Advent Prayer

Song: "O Come, O Come, Emmanuel"

Leader: Prepare the way for our God.
All: Come, Jesus, come.

Group 1: Jesus, as we wait for Your coming, we will try to be fair and just.
Leader: Prepare the way for our God.
All: Come, Jesus, come.

Group 2: Jesus, as we wait for Your coming, we will care for the sick and the poor.
Leader: Prepare the way for our God.
All: Come, Jesus, come.

Group 3: Jesus, as we wait for Your coming, we will try to be peacemakers.
Leader: Prepare the way for our God.
All: Come, Jesus, come.

Song: "O Come, O Come, Emmanuel"

REVIEW ■ TEST

Circle the letter beside the correct answer.

1. The Church's special time of waiting to celebrate Jesus' birth is
   a. Christmas.   **b.** All Souls.   **c.** Advent.

2. In ancient times prophets told the people to prepare for the
   a. Savior.   **b.** resurrection.   **c.** Church.

3. There are _____ weeks in the season of Advent.
   a. three   **b.** four   **c.** five

4. During Advent, the priest wears _____ vestments.
   a. white   **b.** purple   **c.** green

5. What will you do to care for the poor this Advent?

   _____

   _____

FAITH ALIVE   AT HOME AND IN THE PARISH

In this lesson your child learned more about the season of Advent. Advent is a time of waiting during which we prepare to celebrate the coming of Jesus, our God and Savior. For Christians, Advent symbolizes the long years God's people waited for the Messiah. The prophets taught them to prepare by praying, caring for the poor, making peace, and being just to everyone.

Acts of Kindness

Encourage your family to do acts of kindness for others as one way to prepare for the coming of Jesus. If you wish, hang up a Christmas stocking for Jesus. Invite family members to put a paper heart or other symbol inside each time they perform an act of kindness. On Christmas, offer the stocking as your family gift to Jesus.

†Invitation to Praise God

Pray this psalm with your family during Advent.

Yes, God is good.
God's love is eternal.
God's faithfulness lasts forever.
From Psalm 100:5

Learn by heart   Faith Summary

- Jesus came to be our Savior.
- During Advent we prepare to celebrate Jesus' birth and wait for Him to come again in glory.

14 Christmas

O Holy Child of Bethlehem, come into our hearts.

OUR LIFE

Joseph and Mary went to Bethlehem to be enrolled in the census ordered by Caesar Augustus. While they were there, Jesus was born. Mary wrapped Him in swaddling clothes and laid Him in a manger, because there was no room for them in the inn.

An angel of the Lord appeared to some shepherds and said, "Do not be afraid. I bring you good news of great joy for all people. The Savior has been born."
From Luke 2:1–11

What do you like best about this Christmas story?
What is the "good news" of Christmas for you?

SHARING LIFE

Tell why you think we share gifts at Christmas.

Imagine that you have moved to a new country. You don't know anyone and you can't speak the language. What would be the best gift you could receive there?

Tell how Jesus is God's special gift to you.

132

On the first Christmas, God gave us the gift of Jesus. The best gifts we can give at Christmas are the gifts of ourselves.

Is there someone you would like to give a special gift to at Christmas?

- Close your eyes and picture that person.

- Think about a gift you can give. (Remember, it should not cost money or come from a store.)

- Imagine yourself giving your gift to that person. How do you feel?

Pray with your friends,

† Thank You, God, for the gift of Jesus. Help us to give the gifts of ourselves at Christmas and all year long.

We Will Learn

- God's greatest gift to us is God's own son, Jesus Christ.

- At Christmas we celebrate the birth of Jesus.

We Celebrate Jesus' Birth

God's greatest gift to us is God's own Son, Jesus Christ. At Christmas we celebrate Jesus' birth in a stable in Bethlehem.

A long time ago, Saint Francis of Assisi wanted to help people understand better the story of Jesus' birth. He had a wonderful idea!

He gathered the townspeople together. Two of them pretended to be Mary and Joseph. A little baby boy was placed in the manger, the box from which animals ate. Real oxen and a donkey were brought in.

Then at midnight on Christmas Eve, Francis invited all the people to come to the stable. How surprised and full of wonder they were. They prayed and sang songs around this first "live" Christmas crib. People liked it so much that the custom spread all over the world.

At Christmas time, you will see a Christmas crib somewhere in your church. It will have statues instead of real people. In some parishes a statue of the infant Jesus is carried into church before the first Christmas Mass and placed in the manger as everyone sings a Christmas carol.

The Christmas crib and Christmas carols have become two of the most loved customs of this great feast of Christmas.

Coming to Faith

Work together with a small group of friends.

Practice telling the story of Saint Francis, who made the first Christmas crib. Then tell it to your families.

Sing your favorite Christmas carol together.

PRACTICING FAITH

A Christmas Celebration

All sing: "O Come, All Ye Faithful"

Scene 1: Shepherds on the hillside.

Reader 1: Some shepherds were spending the night in the fields with their sheep. An angel appeared to them in great glory, and they were frightened. The angel said: "Don't be afraid. I bring you good news. Today a Savior has been born for you." Suddenly, a whole chorus of angels appeared and sang.

All sing: Glory to God in the highest, and peace on earth to those with whom God is pleased.

Scene 2: The shepherds come to the stable.

Reader 2: The shepherds said to one another, "Let's go over to Bethlehem and find the child." So they hurried off and found Mary and Joseph and saw the baby Jesus lying in a manger.

Scene 3: The shepherds stand or kneel before the manger. Mary and Joseph show them Jesus.

All sing: "Silent Night"

Talk with your teacher about ways you and your family might use the "Faith Alive" section. Talk to your family about making gifts of love for one another at Christmas.

REVIEW · TEST

Complete each sentence.

1. The custom of the Christmas crib was begun by Saint _____.

2. A carol we sing at Christmas is " _____."

3. God's greatest gift to us is _____.

4. Jesus was born in a _____.

5. How will you show you are grateful for the gift of Jesus?

_____

_____

_____

FAITH ALIVE AT HOME AND IN THE PARISH

In this lesson your child learned about the true meaning of Christmas. The Christmas liturgies celebrate God's promise kept and human expectation fulfilled. The gospels recall the story of Jesus' birth, and familiar Christmas carols repeat the message of God's love for us during the Christmas season.

Gifts of Love

Talk with your family about the true spirit of Christmas. Emphasize that what makes Christmas gifts special is not their size or cost; rather it is the love with which the gifts are given. Invite your family to give gifts of love to one another at Christmas. Place the names of all family members in a bag or box. Have each person draw a name and make a gift of love for that person. Ideas: a letter or poem expressing feelings about the person; breakfast in bed for Mom or Dad; a homemade album of photos or drawings about the family.

Christmas Carols

If possible, plan an old-fashioned sing-along around the Christmas tree, with all family members selecting the carols. If you wish, make copies of the lyrics and bind them in booklets with festive handmade covers. Consider contacting friends about forming a group to carol on Christmas Eve.

Learn by heart **Faith Summary**

- God's greatest gift to us is God's own Son, Jesus Christ.

- At Christmas we celebrate the birth of Jesus.

15 Our Church and the Bible

God, Your word
is a light for
our lives!

OUR LIFE

A long, long time ago before there was such a thing as writing, people passed on what they knew and had been taught through stories and spoken accounts.

They would sit around the campfire at night while the storyteller told exciting stories about the beginning of the world, animals, and people. People remembered the stories and told them again and again down through the years.

Which stories have you read over and over again? Tell about them.

Does your family have special stories? Why are these stories so special?

SHARING LIFE

What stories do you like best?

What would life be like without good stories?

What are your favorite stories about God and about our Church?

Form small groups. Imagine you are sitting around a campfire. Share with one another these stories from the Bible.

Think about the stories you have shared. Which one did you like best? Decorate that footprint. Then tell what you learned from this story for your own life.

In this lesson we will discover that the Bible is the wonderful story of God's love for us and our call to live as God's people.

Pentecost

Jesus and the Children

The Forgiving Father

The Last Supper

We Will Learn

- The Bible is the the story of God's love for us.

- In the gospels we read stories about what Jesus said and did.

- Catholics love and respect the Bible.

139

■ Thank You, God, for giving us stories that teach us about Your love for us.

■ Share something that you have learned from the Bible.

The Bible, the Word of God

Our Church has a wonderful story to tell. It is the true story of God's love for us and how we are called to live as God's people. The great book of this story is the Bible.

The Bible story began thousands of years ago when God called Abraham and Sarah. They were to leave their own country for a new land that later would be called Israel. Their descendants who settled there were called Israelites.

God chose the Israelites from all the other nations on earth to be God's own people. God promised to watch over and bless them forever. The Israelites promised to live as God's own people.

The Jewish people today come from this Israelite family. We share with them our faith in the one true God.

For hundreds of years the Israelites wrote down stories of what God was doing for them. We find these stories in the first part of the Bible, called the Old Testament.

In time, God's own Son came among us. Jesus was born a Jew and grew up in the land of the Israelites. He learned the stories of the Jewish people.

He also had a new story to tell them from God. Jesus told them that He had come to bring the good news of God's kingdom to people of every race and nation.

We read about Jesus and His mission in the second part of the Bible. It is called the New Testament.

We listen to stories from the Bible to hear God's word for our lives. We should show great respect for the Bible by listening carefully when it is read. The Church helps us to understand the Bible.

What are the two parts of the Bible?

How can you show respect for the Bible?

OUR CATHOLIC FAITH

■ Loving God, help us to listen to Your word and learn from You.

■ With a partner, share a favorite story about Jesus.

Jesus and Lazarus

The New Testament

When the Church began, the disciples of Jesus met to share the Eucharist and help one another. They shared stories about Jesus and what it meant to live as His disciples. With the help of the Holy Spirit, their stories were written down and passed on to us in the New Testament, the second part of the Bible.

In the New Testament we find the gospels of Matthew, Mark, Luke, and John. In the gospels we read what Jesus said about God's love for us and what He did to show us this love.

Early disciples of Jesus

Gospel is a word that means good news.

The four gospels have many miracle stories. Miracles are special works that Jesus did, such as healing sick people. Jesus even brought His friend Lazarus back to life. Jesus could work miracles because He was the Son of God. We often hear miracle stories in the gospel reading at Mass.

In the gospels we also read the parables. Parables are stories Jesus told to teach us how to do God's will and live as His disciples.

Do you remember the story of the good shepherd? In this story Jesus taught that God loves and cares for everyone—the big and the small, the lost and the found.

Find and write the names of the gospel writers.

_____

_____

_____

_____

■ What have you learned from your favorite gospel story?

■ Will you share with a friend what you have learned? When?

The Good Shepherd

HOLY BIBLE

Dear Jesus, open our hearts to live as Your loving disciples.

What is some good news you have learned from Jesus?

The Church Grows

The good news of Jesus spread quickly. In the part of the New Testament called the Acts of the Apostles, we read stories about the early Church and how it grew. The New Testament also has letters of Saint Paul and other early disciples. The letters explained the good news of Jesus and how to live as His disciples.

Catholics show respect and love for both the Old and New Testaments of the Bible. When we read or listen carefully to the Bible, we know that God is speaking to us to show us how to live our lives today.

God's Word at Mass

Every Sunday at Mass we hear God's word from the Bible during the Liturgy of the Word.

The first reading at Mass is most often from the Old Testament. The second reading is from the New Testament, but not from one of the four gospels. The third reading is always from one of the four gospels (Matthew, Mark, Luke, or John).

The Bible readings for each Mass are chosen by the Church to help us celebrate each Sunday and season of the Church year. The book that has all the readings we use at Mass is called the *Lectionary*. It is not the whole Bible, but it contains parts of the Bible.

The person who reads the first two readings is called the lector. The word *lector* means "reader." The priest or deacon reads the gospel. Will you listen carefully to the readings at Mass this Sunday?

You might invite your family to talk together about the Sunday readings either before or after Mass.

Learn by heart ### Faith Summary

- The first part of the Bible is called the Old Testament.

- The second part of the Bible is called the New Testament.

- In the gospels of Matthew, Mark, Luke, and John, we read what Jesus did to show us God's love.

COMING TO FAITH

Decide together what the best way is to listen to the Bible, both in church and at home with your family.

Talk together about your favorite stories of Jesus from the New Testament. Act out one of them together.

PRACTICING FAITH

Think quietly about your favorite story of Jesus. Imagine He is with you. What do you think He is asking you to do? Will you do it?

As a group, gather around the Bible. Open to the story you acted out together. Choose one person to hold the Bible up while the group prays the following prayer.

† Dear God,
Thank You for helping us know more about Jesus. Open our hearts to Your word each day. Speak, and we will listen to hear Your will for us.

Talk with your teacher about ways you and your family might use the "Faith Alive" section. Invite your family to do the Family Album activity.

146

REVIEW ∙ TEST

Circle the correct answer.

1. The part of the Bible that tells about the Israelite people is the

New Testament.   Good News.   Old Testament.

2. The part of the Bible that tells about Jesus directly is the

New Testament.   Psalms.   Old Testament.

3. Matthew, Mark, Luke, and John are considered authors of the

Old Testament.   Gospels.   New Testament.

4. The father of the Israelite people was

Abraham.   Isaiah.   Aaron.

5. How can you make the Bible more important in your life?

_____

_____

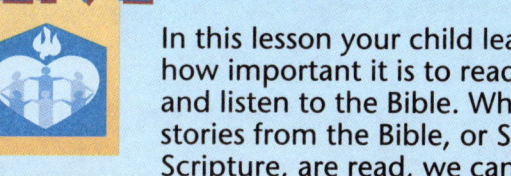

FAITH ALIVE AT HOME AND IN THE PARISH

In this lesson your child learned how important it is to read and listen to the Bible. When stories from the Bible, or Sacred Scripture, are read, we can hear God's word for our lives today. Guided by the Church, we should impart to young people a truly Catholic understanding of the Bible. It is important to avoid the extremes of fundamentalism and literalism. When we follow the Church's guidance, we will certainly do this.

To develop a lifelong love for reading the Bible, your child needs the example of your family. He or she needs to see you quietly meditating on the words of Scripture to gather strength, to regain peace, and to find the ways to live as a disciple of Jesus.

Family Album

If you have a family album, share it with your child. Talk about the importance of preserving family stories and memories. Compare the album to the Bible, which records stories and other memories of God's people. Provide examples from the Old Testament, such as the stories of Moses and the burning bush (Exodus 3:1–22), Ruth and Naomi (Ruth 1:1–22), and David and Goliath (1 Samuel 17:12–54), as well as your favorite parables of Jesus from the New Testament.

Listening to the Bible

Each week share the gospel reading for the coming Sunday. Ask one family member to read the gospel aloud. Give each person an opportunity to tell what Jesus is saying to us in the reading. Then decide as a family how you will try to live God's word.

Jesus, we are Your disciples. Help us to tell others about You.

Our Life

After His death and resurrection, Jesus appeared many times to His disciples. Then He told them to meet Him on a certain mountain in Galilee. There was great excitement among the disciples. When all were assembled, Jesus said to them:

"Go into the whole world and make disciples of all people. Baptize them in the name of the Father, and of the Son, and of the Holy Spirit. Teach them to carry out everything I have told you. And remember that I am with you always until the end of the world."
From Matthew 28:16–20

Name some of the disciples you know today.

Who are the ones who teach you about Jesus?

Sharing Life

Imagine you are on the mountain listening to Jesus. What do you hear Him saying to you?

Talk together about ways your group can be Jesus' disciples right now.

When we live as Jesus' disciples, we show others what it means to live the good news of Jesus.

Think of a time when you lived the good news. Write on the sunburst what you did and why. Then share your good news with one another.

In this lesson we will learn how the Church brings the good news of Jesus to people all over the world.

We Will Learn

- The first Christians shared the good news of Jesus.
- Today the Church shares the good news everywhere.
- We share the good news of Jesus every day.

■ Thank You, Jesus, for helping us to live Your good news.

■ When you hear good news, do you want to share it with others? Tell why.

The Good News Spreads

The first Christians just couldn't keep the good news of Jesus to themselves! The good news is that God is with us and loves us always. The good news is that Jesus is our friend and will always help us to follow His way and to do God's will.

Not everyone was happy to hear the good news of Jesus. People knew they would have to change their lives to follow Jesus' way. Some people did not want to change. They got angry and attacked the first Christians.

Some of Jesus' disciples were dragged out of their homes and put in jail. Others had to hide or run for their lives. Stephen, one of these first Christians, was killed because he preached the good news of Jesus.

A **missionary** is someone who carries the good news of Jesus Christ to others.

At this time, there was a man named Saul who at first hated the disciples of Jesus. One day, a great light from the sky flashed around him. He heard a voice saying, "Saul, Saul! Why do you hurt Me?"

When Saul asked who was speaking, the voice answered, "I am Jesus, whom you are hurting."
From Acts of the Apostles 9:1–5

After this, Saul changed his whole life. He became a Christian and was called Paul. He spent the rest of his life traveling to many lands to spread the good news of Jesus. Paul was a great missionary.

Today the Church has missionaries who carry Jesus' good news to people all over the world. You, too, can bring the good news to your family, your friends, and to other people in your parish.

■ Explain how the early Christians shared the good news.

■ Whom will you tell about Jesus' good news? Why?

OUR CATHOLIC FAITH

■ Jesus, give us the courage to bring the good news of God's love to everyone we meet.

■ Talk about times when you find it difficult to follow Jesus' way.

The Good News Today

It was not always easy for the first Christians to live and share the good news, but they never stopped trying.

Missionaries in our Church today continue in a special way what Paul and the first Christians did. They love God so much they sometimes leave their homes, their families, and their friends to travel to faraway lands.

They teach people about Jesus and show them how to live as disciples of Jesus. They celebrate Mass and the sacraments with them. They respect people of other lands and languages. They share with them ways to love one another, to be fair, and to live in peace.

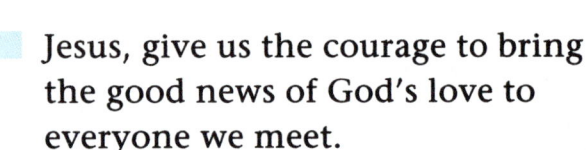

Some missionaries are ordained priests or deacons, and some are married or single lay people. Some missionaries belong to religious communities. They are called religious sisters and brothers.

Missionaries serve as nurses, doctors, and teachers. By their lives of service, they show what it means to live the good news of Jesus.

Missionaries, both here at home and in other lands, are very special people in the Church. They help us in bringing the good news of Jesus to others. Missionaries need our prayers, our letters of encouragement, and our help.

Help a missionary.
Tell what you will do.

_____

_____

_____

_____

Explain how you can be a missionary.

Together write a prayer for missionaries. When will you say this prayer?

153

OUR CATHOLIC FAITH

- Thank You, Jesus, for calling people to be missionaries.

- Can you be a missionary today? Tell how.

The Good News in Our Parishes

Everyone in our Church is called to share the good news of Jesus Christ. We do not have to go to faraway lands. We can be missionaries in our homes, in our school, and in our parish.

We can spread the good news by:

- sharing the Catholic faith when we have the chance to do so.

- letting others see how hard we try each day to live the Law of Love.

- reaching out to help the sick, the poor, or those who are treated unfairly.

- being peacemakers, and by praying with others that God's kingdom will be lived everywhere in the world.

Name some things that people in your parish do to spread the good news.

Missionaries

Before Jesus left His disciples, He told them to go to all peoples everywhere and make them His followers, too. Remembering this, the Church has always sent missionaries to bring the good news of Jesus to the whole world. Saint Paul soon became one of the most famous missionaries. Many centuries later, another great missionary, Saint Francis Xavier, was named a patron saint of the missions. Since the time of Jesus, many other men and women have brought the good news to peoples around the world.

Imagine you are preparing to be a missionary in a faraway country. What do you think you would need to learn before you could share the good news of Jesus with the people?

Missionaries need our help. They need us to pray for them. Would you like to adopt a missionary for whom you can pray each day? Talk with your group about how to do this.

Learn by heart **Faith Summary**

- The first Christians spread the good news of Jesus Christ.

- Today missionaries bring the good news to people everywhere.

- Everyone in our Church is called to share the good news of Jesus.

COMING TO FAITH

Divide into three groups.

Talk about ways you can be missionaries of Jesus' good news at home, in your neighborhood, and in your parish.

PRACTICING FAITH

Make a television set together.

- Cut a square in one side of a large carton.

- Cut a slit in each of the corresponding sides.

Work together to create a TV program telling some of the good news of Jesus. Draw pictures on 8½" x 11" paper. Tape the pictures together in order. Then write a script to go with the pictures. When your program is ready, thread the paper through the slits to go across the "screen" as someone reads the script.

Talk with your teacher about ways you and your family might use the "Faith Alive" section. Invite your family to choose a way to show that you are missionaries of Jesus' good news.

156

REVIEW ▪ TEST

Circle **T** for **True** or **F** for **False**.
If you are not sure, circle **?**.

1. Stephen was killed because he preached the
   good news of Jesus.   T   F   ?

2. Paul was a great missionary in the Church.   T   F   ?

3. Missionaries only go to foreign lands.   T   F   ?

4. Missionaries need our help.   T   F   ?

5. Write one way you could help a missionary this week.

_____

_____

_____

FAITH ALIVE — AT HOME AND IN THE PARISH

In this lesson your child learned that all Catholics can be missionaries and spread the good news of Jesus to others in their schools, parishes, and neighborhoods.

Missionaries, both here at home and in other lands, are very special people in the Church. Because they often are far away, they can sometimes feel forgotten. Explain that missionaries need our prayers, our letters of encouragement, and our help.

Discuss the fact that we do not have to go to faraway lands to tell others the good news. We can be missionaries in our homes, in our parishes, and in our neighborhoods.

Ask your parish for the name and address of a missionary. Then decide how your family will help this person.

Missionary Family

With your family decide what you can do to show that you are a missionary family. Ideas: call a relative to say "we love you"; visit or send a homemade card to a sick or grieving parishioner; welcome a new neighbor or parish member with home-baked cookies. Plan how each of you will contribute to your missionary project.

† Prayer for Missionaries

Saint Thérèse and Saint Francis Xavier, patrons of all missionaries, help and guide missionaries today. Help the members of our families to be missionaries, too.

17   Our Church as a Community

*Loving Jesus,
help us to love
one another as
You love us.*

Our Life

The fire raged quickly across the dry hills. People living in the canyon area barely had time to save themselves. Cara watched the television news with her parents. She was happy that the fire had not been near their home.

The next day at Mass, Father Martin said, "Many of our friends and neighbors are in great need today. If you'd like to help, meet me and our parish outreach team in the parish center after Mass."

Cara went with her parents and many other parishioners to see what they could do. Soon all were involved in plans to find housing, food, and clothing for the fire victims. Cara was proud of her parish community.

Can you name ways your parish works together? How do you help?

Sharing Life

Work together with your friends. List all the things third graders can do in your parish.

Share how you feel about belonging to a parish community.

Work with a partner to complete this puzzle.

1. Trace the puzzle on a piece of paper.

2. Cut out the puzzle pieces.

3. On each piece, write how you feel about belonging to your parish community.

4. Exchange your puzzle pieces with a friend. The challenge is to complete someone else's puzzle.

Share all the puzzles within your group. Then decide:

● Is everyone in a parish important? Why?

● Why do we need to help one another in our parish?

In this lesson we will explore how everyone in the Church is challenged to carry on Jesus' mission.

How We Feel About Belonging to Our Parish

We Will Learn

● There are people who lead and serve the Church.

● A vocation is each person's invitation to serve God and the Church in a special way.

● By Baptism we are called to carry on the mission of Jesus.

- Thank You, Jesus, for my parish community.
- Why do you think we need to belong to a parish?

Those Who Lead and Serve

The Catholic Church is a community guided by the Holy Spirit. The Church has spread all over the world. Everywhere it works to build up the kingdom, or reign, of God.

Our Holy Father, the pope, is the bishop of Rome and the leader of the whole Catholic Church. He teaches us about our faith, helps us to live the good news, and helps us to build up God's reign.

Name our pope.

_____

Catholic parishes are grouped together into dioceses. Each diocese has a bishop as its leader and teacher. The Holy Spirit helps the bishop to serve the people of the diocese and to bring them together.

Name your bishop.

_____

Each diocese has many parishes. Each parish is led by a pastor or an administrator.

Name your pastor.

_____

160

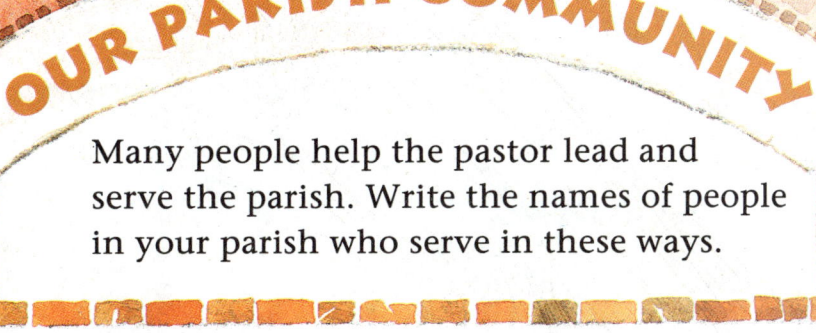

OUR PARISH COMMUNITY

Many people help the pastor lead and serve the parish. Write the names of people in your parish who serve in these ways.

Workers in Our Parish	Names
other **priests**, who celebrate Mass, the sacraments, and teach the good news	
the **Catholic school principal** and the **director of religious education,** who lead teachers, catechists, and young people in learning and living their faith	
full-time **parish workers**, who help to carry on the mission of Jesus (for example, religious sisters or brothers and lay people like your parents and teachers)	
parish council members, chosen by the pastor and people to plan how the parish can spread God's kingdom	
justice and peace workers, who help our parish to work for the kingdom, or reign, of God	

- Explain why we need people to lead and serve the Church.

- What will you do to help serve in your parish?

OUR CATHOLIC FAITH

■ Loving Jesus, bless those who lead and serve the Church.

■ Would you like to serve the Church in a special way some day? Why or why not?

Vocations in the Church

By our Baptism, each of us is invited to carry on Jesus' mission and serve others. A vocation is an invitation to serve God and the Church in a special way. There are many kinds of vocations.

Some people in our Church are called by God to be ordained ministers. They receive the sacrament of Holy Orders. They are bishops, priests, and deacons.

Others are called by God to live as religious sisters or brothers. They live in religious communities and serve in many ways.

Sometimes lay people choose to work full-time carrying on Jesus' mission. They are called pastoral ministers.

Many women and men are called by God to the vocation of marriage. They share their life and love with each other and with their children. They spread the good news by living holy lives, as Jesus did.

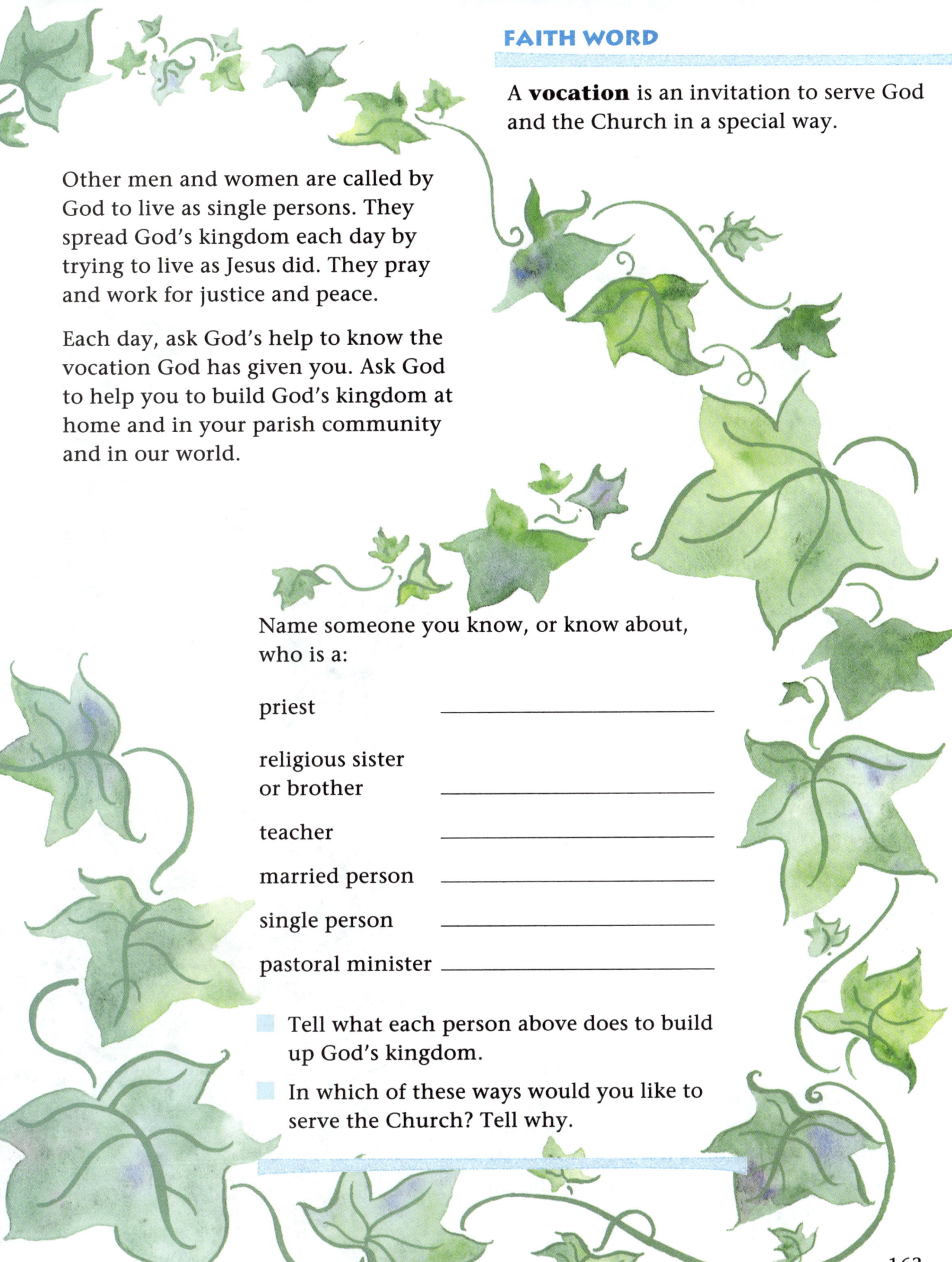

A **vocation** is an invitation to serve God and the Church in a special way.

Other men and women are called by God to live as single persons. They spread God's kingdom each day by trying to live as Jesus did. They pray and work for justice and peace.

Each day, ask God's help to know the vocation God has given you. Ask God to help you to build God's kingdom at home and in your parish community and in our world.

Name someone you know, or know about, who is a:

priest _____

religious sister
or brother _____

teacher _____

married person _____

single person _____

pastoral minister _____

Tell what each person above does to build up God's kingdom.

In which of these ways would you like to serve the Church? Tell why.

163

OUR CATHOLIC FAITH

Holy Spirit, help me to know the vocation You want me to follow.

Do you think God may be calling you to a special vocation? Which one?

Our Family in the Church

The family is a very important part of the Church community. It is in our family that we first learn about God, the good news of Jesus, and the Church. In our family we learn to love, to make peace, and to be fair.

Sometimes people in our family feel angry, sad, sick, or lonely. We should always try to love and help them. We should talk to one another about our hurts and our joys. We should pray together for God's help.

If you are not happy, talk to your parents, a teacher, a priest, or some other grown-up friend. Tell them how you feel and ask for their help. Jesus does not want you to hold your hurts inside you. He wants you and your family to be happy.

Your family is a very important part of the parish. Every family should help the parish to become the kind of community Jesus wants. We are a community of people who worship God together. We are a community that loves and cares for each of its members.

Choosing a New Pope

When a pope dies, the cardinals of the Church gather at the Vatican in Rome. They come from all over the world to elect a new pope.

The cardinals meet in the Sistine Chapel. There they pray together to ask the Holy Spirit to guide them in choosing the next pope. Then the election begins. This is done by secret ballot. The ballots are burned after each vote. If a new pope has not been chosen, something is put on the ballots to make the smoke black. When white smoke rises from the chimney, people know that a new pope has been elected.

Crowds gather outside the Vatican to cheer for the new pope. Catholics throughout the world pray for and celebrate their new leader.

Imagine you are in the crowd. How do you feel as you see white smoke rising? What prayer can you say for the pope today?

Pope John XXIII

Pope John Paul I

Learn by heart

Faith Summary

- The pope, bishops, and pastors lead and serve our Church.

- By Baptism we are called to carry on the mission of Jesus.

- A vocation is an invitation to serve God and the Church in a special way.

165

Coming To Faith

You, too, have a part to play in our Church!

Tell what you can do and how you can work for God's kingdom.

Practicing Faith

Talk to your parents and to priests, brothers, sisters, and single people you know. Find out how they work for God's kingdom in their vocations.

Pray together for all people who are trying to answer God's call to serve others. Some may be struggling with a decision to marry or stay single. Others may be trying to find out whether God is calling them to the religious life as a sister or brother, or to the ordained ministry of deacon or priest. Say together:

† Loving God, may Your Spirit be with all who try to do Your will. We pray, too, that we will listen to the Holy Spirit. May we always live to do Your will. Amen.

Talk with your teacher about ways you and your family might use the "Faith Alive" section. Share with your family what you learned about vocations in the Church.

REVIEW ■ TEST

Complete the sentences below.

1. The Bishop of Rome and the leader of the whole Catholic Church is

_____.

2. The person who leads and serves the parish, sometimes with the help of a parish council, is the

_____.

3. The person who leads and serves the people of his diocese is the

_____.

4. Everyone in the Church is called to spread the

_____.

5. Tell one way you can try to live a holy life.

_____

_____

FAITH ALIVE AT HOME AND IN THE PARISH

In this lesson your child learned more about the Catholic Church community—its people, ministries, and organization around the world. But you must show him or her that the family is the most important part of the Church community. Your family is the first and best place for your child to learn about God, the Church, and the good news of Jesus. In your family your child learns to love and serve others.

Teach the family members to reach out to help and to share their hurts and joys. Be sure to pray together as a family—for example, in the morning and at bedtime, as well as before and after meals.

Choosing a Vocation

Ask your child to share what he or she has learned about vocations in the Church. Discuss the importance of seeking help from God and advice from others in choosing a vocation. Help your child write a prayer to ask God's guidance in choosing a vocation, or use this prayer: "Loving God, help me to know what You want me to do. Show me how to spread Your kingdom and grow in love for You."

The Family's Vocation

Gather with your family to thank God for the gift of your vocation. Ask God to bless your family and to help you reach out to families in need. Then plan specific ways to do this, such as the giving of time, food, or clothing.

18 Our Church Works for Justice and Peace

Jesus, help us to work for peace in our homes and neighborhoods.

Our Life

In Jesus' time, just as today, there were people who were not treated fairly.

Peter, the leader of the apostles, sometimes stayed in the homes of Gentiles to tell them Jesus' good news. Gentiles were people who were not Jewish.

Some people in the Church did not like Gentiles and did not want them to belong to their Church. But Peter baptized Gentiles and welcomed them into Jesus' community.

Some of Peter's Christian friends were angry with him. They said, "You were a guest in the home of Gentiles, and you even ate with them!"
From Acts of the Apostles 11:3

Peter reminded the first Christians that because everyone is equal in the eyes of God, Jesus wants us to treat all people with love, respect, and fairness.

Do you know people who are treated unfairly? Tell about it.

Sharing Life

When you hear about or see someone in your neighborhood or school treated unfairly, how does it make you feel? Why are people sometimes treated unfairly?

Act out some ways God wants us to treat people.

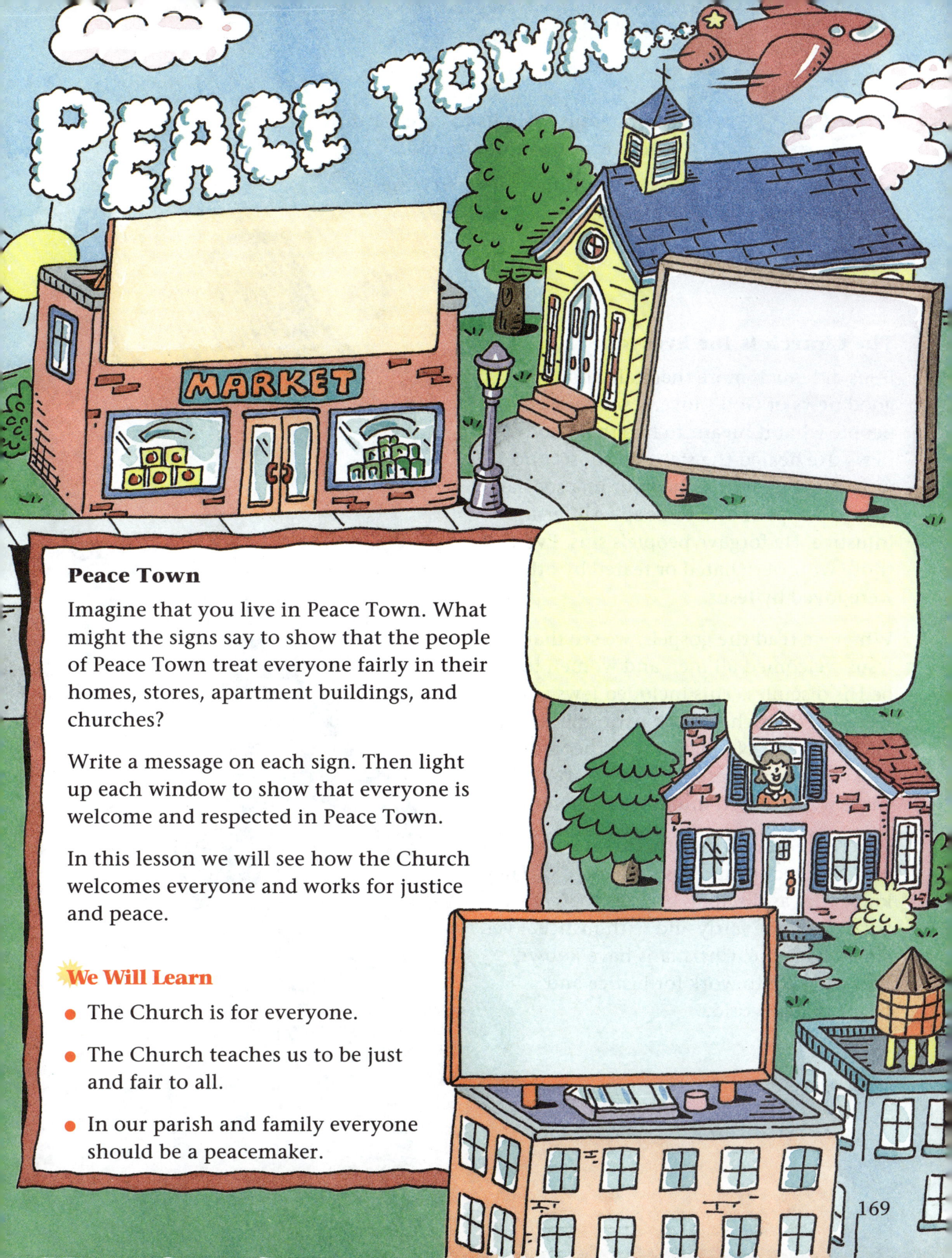

PEACE TOWN...

Peace Town

Imagine that you live in Peace Town. What might the signs say to show that the people of Peace Town treat everyone fairly in their homes, stores, apartment buildings, and churches?

Write a message on each sign. Then light up each window to show that everyone is welcome and respected in Peace Town.

In this lesson we will see how the Church welcomes everyone and works for justice and peace.

We Will Learn

- The Church is for everyone.
- The Church teaches us to be just and fair to all.
- In our parish and family everyone should be a peacemaker.

169

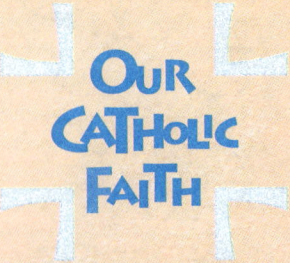

OUR CATHOLIC FAITH

- Loving Jesus, help us to care for those who are treated unfairly today.
- Tell something you do to treat people fairly.

The Church Is for Everyone

Jesus did much more than talk about the good news of God's love. Jesus showed people what it meant to live that good news. He healed the sick and those who were hurting. He reached out in a special way to the poor and to people suffering injustice. He forgave people's sins. Even those who were hated or feared by others were loved by Jesus.

When we read the gospels, we see that Jesus welcomed all men and women to be His disciples. This included Jews and Gentiles, the rich and the poor, the strong and the weak. No matter what people looked like or where they came from, all of them were invited into Jesus' community.

When the Church began, the first disciples remembered what Jesus said and did. They knew that as disciples of Jesus they must treat everyone fairly and with justice. Ever since that time, Christians have known that they are to work for justice and peace in our world.

170

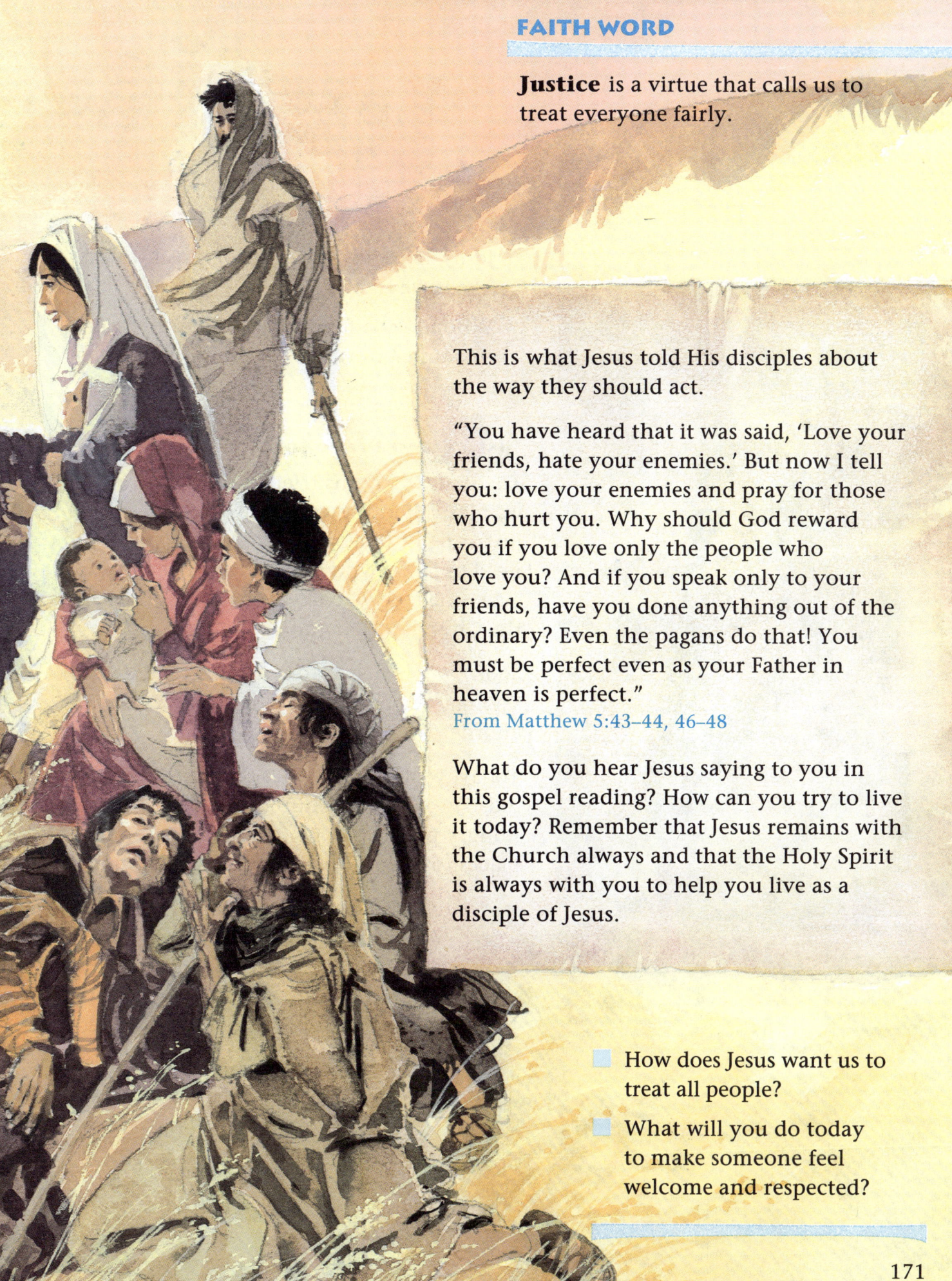

Justice is a virtue that calls us to treat everyone fairly.

This is what Jesus told His disciples about the way they should act.

"You have heard that it was said, 'Love your friends, hate your enemies.' But now I tell you: love your enemies and pray for those who hurt you. Why should God reward you if you love only the people who love you? And if you speak only to your friends, have you done anything out of the ordinary? Even the pagans do that! You must be perfect even as your Father in heaven is perfect."
From Matthew 5:43–44, 46–48

What do you hear Jesus saying to you in this gospel reading? How can you try to live it today? Remember that Jesus remains with the Church always and that the Holy Spirit is always with you to help you live as a disciple of Jesus.

- How does Jesus want us to treat all people?

- What will you do today to make someone feel welcome and respected?

171

Justice

■ Jesus, help me to treat others as I would like to be treated.

■ Who in your family needs your help at this time? How can you help that person?

Justice and Peace for All

The first Christians tried hard to live the way Jesus had shown them. They tried to be just and fair to all people, especially those in need or those who felt left out. They made everyone feel welcome in Jesus' community, the Church.

Soon, others began to notice. People started saying, "See how these Christians love one another."

Today, we try to do what the first Christians did. The Catholic Church has places where hungry people can go for food. We set up places to sleep for those who have no homes.

In some parts of the world, people do not even have clothes to wear. Our Church tries to help them, too. Our Church asks people who have more than they need to share with others.

The popes have often written and reminded us that Catholics must defend the rights of people who are treated unfairly. When we treat all people fairly, we are God's peacemakers.

and Peace

The Catholic bishops in the United States have written important letters about peace and about treating people fairly. In these letters, they tell our country's leaders and all of us that we are called to work for justice and peace in our world.

Making peace begins with each one of us. All the followers of Jesus must be peacemakers. When we are just and fair to everyone we meet, we begin to build a family, a parish, and a world in which all can live in peace.

Saint Francis of Assisi

Francis left the rich home of his parents and gave all he owned to the poor. Francis became known as a great peacemaker. He wrote a beautiful prayer for peace. We celebrate his feast day on October 4.

Find Saint Francis's prayer for peace on page 175. Write the lines that you like best.

_____

_____

◼ What does the Church teach us about being peacemakers?

◼ How will you be fair to someone others do not like?

173

OUR CATHOLIC FAITH

■ Holy Spirit, help me to treat all people justly.

■ Think about a time when you acted as a peacemaker. Tell about it.

Peacemakers in Our Parish

Everyone in our parish should be a peacemaker. Look around your parish and see what some people do to be peacemakers.

Some people are peacemakers when they visit and care for the sick or help older people. Others help disabled people and make sure that they are treated fairly. This means that those who have some disability are treated like everyone else.

There are parishes that welcome refugees, those who must run away from their own countries because of injustice. These parishes help them to find homes, learn to speak our language, and get jobs.

Others in our parish work to put an end to war and bring about an end to violence.

Everyone who looks at our parish should want to say, "See how these Christians love other people." Everyone should be able to call us a parish of justice and peace.

JUSTICE AND PEACE

An Instrument of Christ's Peace

Saint Francis of Assisi was a great peacemaker. In a wonderful way, he showed us what it means to follow the way of Jesus.

Francis tried to live as Jesus lived. Francis freely chose a simple life, caring for the sick and the poor. Wherever he went, he preached the good news of God's love. He often greeted people, saying, "May our Lord give you peace."

Like Jesus, Francis attracted many followers. He founded a religious community called the Franciscans. To this day, the Franciscans continue to follow the way of Jesus and bring Christ's peace to those in need.

Read again the prayer of Saint Francis. Then turn back to page 173 where you wrote the lines you like best.

Think: How can you put those prayer words into practice today and show others that you follow the way of Jesus?

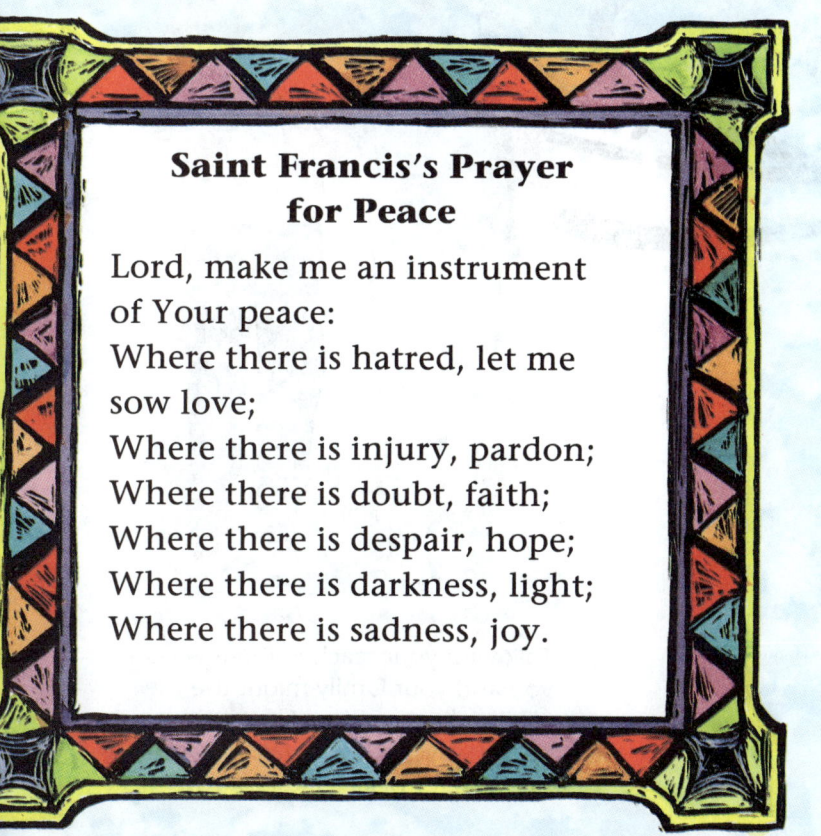

Saint Francis's Prayer for Peace

Lord, make me an instrument
of Your peace:
Where there is hatred, let me
sow love;
Where there is injury, pardon;
Where there is doubt, faith;
Where there is despair, hope;
Where there is darkness, light;
Where there is sadness, joy.

Learn by heart **Faith Summary**

- The Catholic Church welcomes everyone.

- The Church teaches us to be just and fair to all people.

- In our parish, everyone should work for justice and peace.

Coming To Faith

Work with a partner or two to act out how these persons can make peace:

- two friends who are angry with each other.

- a family that is angry because someone from a faraway country moved next door.

- the leaders of two countries who want to go to war.

- a rich person and someone who is hungry.

WORLD PEACE BEGINS WITH ME

Practicing Faith

Divide into groups of three or four to become Peace Patrols!

Plan together one way your group can be peacemakers this week in your parish.

Here's a clue: look for those who are not being treated fairly.

What else will your Peace Patrol do?

Talk with your teacher about ways you and your family might use the "Faith Alive" section. Share with your family ways that your family can be partners for peace and justice.

REVIEW · TEST

Circle **T** for **True** or **F** for **False**.
If you are not sure, circle **?**.

1. The Catholic bishops wrote an important letter about peace.   T   F   ?

2. We should be fair only to people we like.   T   F   ?

3. When we treat all people fairly, we are God's peacemakers.   T   F   ?

4. Our parish should be a community of justice and peace.   T   F   ?

5. Tell why God wants us to treat all people fairly.

_____

_____

_____

FAITH ALIVE AT HOME AND IN THE PARISH

In this lesson your child learned that all people should be welcome in the Church and be treated with respect. There is no room for the sins of racism, sexism, and prejudice among Christians, who are called to love one another. The Catholic Church clearly teaches that our faith requires us to work for justice and peace.

Peace Town

Ask your child to tell you about the picture of Peace Town on page 169 and to explain the messages on the signs. Talk about the ways Peace Town is what Jesus hopes our parish will be like. Everyone should know that we are a parish of peace and justice by the way we live. If possible, mention specific ways your parish works to overcome poverty, discrimination in housing, prejudice, and the like. Then pray Saint Francis's prayer for peace on page 175.

Partners for Peace and Justice

Talk with your family about a current peace and justice issue, such as poverty, racial intolerance, or excessive consumerism. If possible, cite examples from the news media or personal experience. Decide what your family can do to be partners for justice and peace with respect to the issues discussed. Then have your child draw a peace symbol on a sheet of paper. Around the symbol, list what your family will try to do. Display the sheet. From time to time, talk about your family's progress as justice and peace partners.

Loving God,
help us to build
up Your
kingdom.

Our Life

Jesus was so excited about the kingdom of God. He wanted everyone to know what it was like. Here are some things He said.

The kingdom is like a wonderful banquet that a king gave. Everyone was invited to attend.

The kingdom of God is like a great treasure hidden in a field. A person finds it and sells everything to buy the field.
From Matthew 13:44; 22:1–14

What do you think Jesus meant when He said that everyone was invited to the banquet?

For what great treasure would you give all that you have?

Sharing Life

How would you tell someone what the kingdom of God is like?

Finish this sentence.

For me, the kingdom of God is like. . . .

Share your ideas with your friends.

Here is another way to describe living for the kingdom of God.

1. With a partner, list in the treasure chest words that tell what living for God's kingdom, or reign, might be like.

2. Share your word-picture of living for God's kingdom with your group.

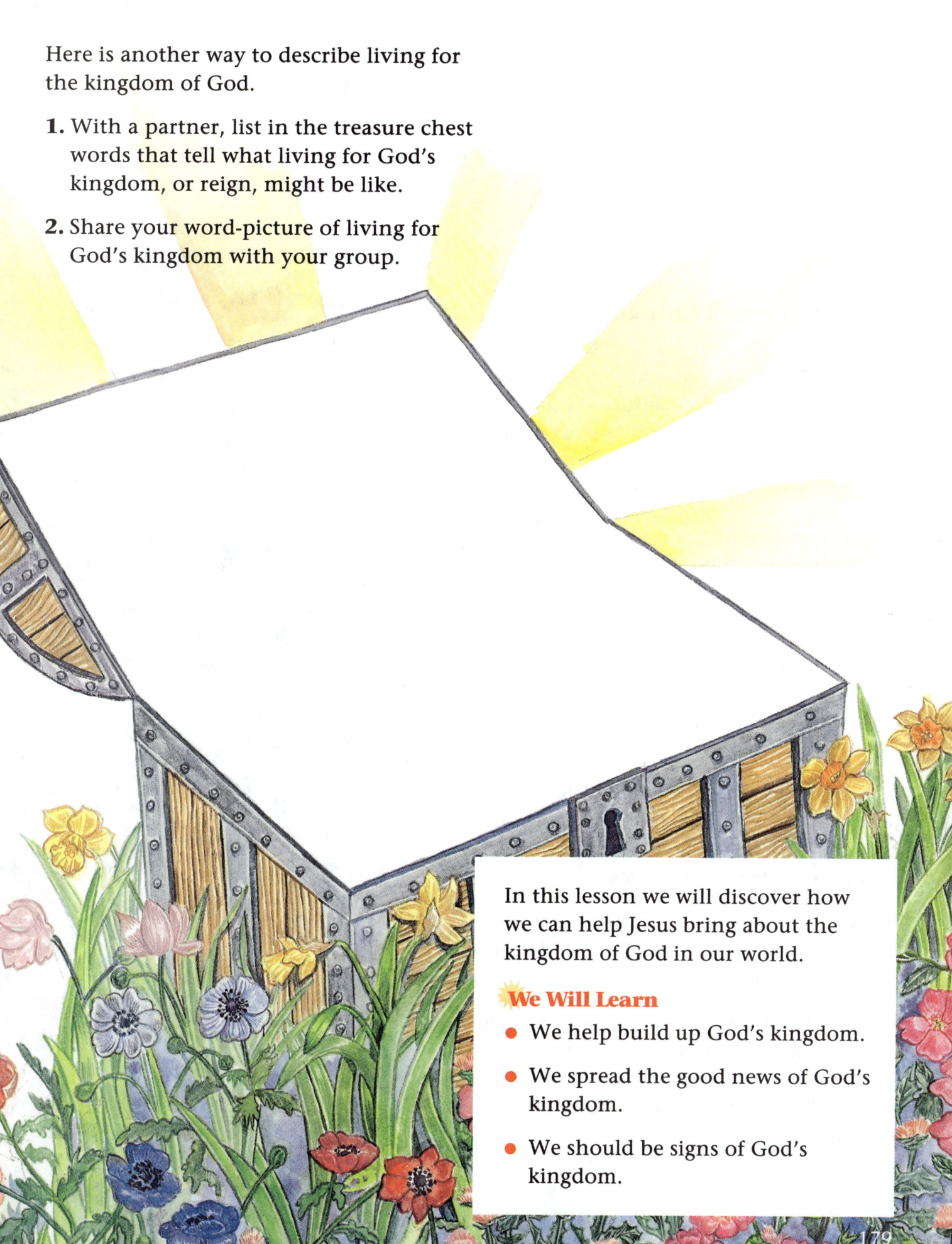

In this lesson we will discover how we can help Jesus bring about the kingdom of God in our world.

We Will Learn

- We help build up God's kingdom.

- We spread the good news of God's kingdom.

- We should be signs of God's kingdom.

OUR CATHOLIC FAITH

■ Jesus, help me to build up God's kingdom by being kind to one person today.

■ Make up your own parable that tells what you think the kingdom, or reign, of God is like.

We Build Up God's Kingdom

Jesus taught His disciples how to work for a world in which people would love, respect, and be fair to everyone. Jesus said that when people live the Law of Love, are just, and try to make peace, they help to build up the kingdom, or reign, of God in the world.

Here is another story, or parable, Jesus told to help us understand more about living and working for God's kingdom.

"The kingdom of God is like this. A man is looking for fine pearls, and when he finds one that is unusually fine, he goes and sells everything he has, and buys that pearl."
From Matthew 13:45–46

Just as He did in the parable of the treasure, Jesus was teaching His disciples that God's kingdom and doing God's loving will must always come first in our lives.

Jesus told another story to show that the kingdom, or reign, of God begins when even one person starts living the Law of Love.

Jesus said, "The kingdom of God is like this. A man takes a mustard seed and plants it in his field. The plant grows and becomes a tree, and all the birds make their nests in its branches."
From Luke 13:19

The **kingdom**, or **reign, of God** is the power of God's life and love in the world.

Many of the people listening to Jesus were farmers. They knew that even though a mustard seed is one of the tiniest seeds, it grows into a large tree.

The message of God's kingdom started out like a small mustard seed. It began with Jesus and a few disciples.

Today the Church has spread Jesus' message all over the world. The Church continues Jesus' work of freeing people from sin and bringing them close to God. Each person, family, parish, and diocese must work together to continue building up God's kingdom in people's hearts. In this way we will bring God's love and justice to our world.

Color the picture of the mustard tree.

- Imagine you are there listening to Jesus. What do you hear Him saying about God's kingdom?

- What will you do today to build the kingdom of God in your family or parish?

◼ Thank You, Father, for all those who show us how to live with love, justice, and peace.

◼ What can you do today to build up the kingdom, or reign, of God?

The Good News of God's Kingdom

Jesus told this story to help us understand that not everyone receives the good news of God's kingdom with an open heart.

Once there was a man who went out to plant some seed. As he scattered the seed in the field, some fell along the side. The birds came and ate it up.

Some fell on rocky ground where there was very little soil. The sun soon dried up the young plants that grew from this seed. Some of the seed fell among thorn bushes that choked the young plants.

But some seed fell on good soil. The plants from this seed grew healthy and large and gave a lot of grain.

From Matthew 13:3–8

Jesus knew that some people would hear the message of God's kingdom and would not accept it. They are like the field where the seed was eaten up by the birds.

The rocky ground stands for those who get very excited when they hear the word of God but then find it too hard to live that word. The message, or seed, never takes root in their hearts.

The thorn bushes stand for those who hear the message of Jesus but let other things crowd it out. They forget to put God first in their lives.

The good soil stands for those who truly hear the message of God's kingdom. Each day they try to live it, no matter what happens. These are the ones who build up God's kingdom of justice, peace, and love.

If we are to help build up God's kingdom, we must be like the good ground. Each day, no matter how hard it is, we must try to bring God's love and peace to at least one other person.

Through you, the power of God's life and love can spread all over the world.

- Act out the parable of the sower.
- Which kind of ground for the seed of God's word will you be? How?

183

OUR CATHOLIC FAITH

■ Jesus, help us to bring God's love and peace to someone today.

■ Choose someone with whom you will share God's love and peace in a special way.

Signs of God's Kingdom

When Jesus taught His disciples to pray, He told them to say, "Thy kingdom come, Thy will be done on earth as it is in heaven." We are signs of God's kingdom, or reign, when we do God's loving will each day.

Like the sower, the Catholic Church today has spread Jesus' message all over the world. But each person, family, parish, and diocese must be a sign of God's kingdom by doing God's loving will for us. When we do God's will, we spread the power of God's life and love all over the world.

When we try to live peacefully with others and treat everyone fairly, we are signs that God is with us.

We try to be cheerful and do what is right, even when it is hard. This shows everyone that we want to be happy now and forever with God in heaven.

Living for God's Kingdom

Did you know that some men and women in the Church spend their entire lives in prayer for God's kingdom? In fact, they are praying for you right now. We call these men and women cloistered nuns and monks.

Only a few people are called by God to this special vocation. They live in convents or monasteries, which they never leave. There they spend each day thinking about God and praying for the coming of God's kingdom—even while they are working. This is how they do God's will and help build up the kingdom of God.

Stop for a moment. Think: Someone may be praying for you right now. How does this make you feel?

How does praying for one another help us build up God's kingdom? Is there someone you would like to pray for today?

Learn by heart Faith Summary

- The kingdom, or reign, of God is the power of God's life and love in the world.

- We all have a part to play in building up the kingdom of God.

- When we do God's will, we are signs of the reign of God.

Coming To Faith

Write what the parable of the sower
and the seed tells you about the kingdom of God.
Draw a symbol that will help you to remember it.

Parable of the Sower

Message   Symbol

_____

_____

_____

Practicing Faith

Circle one of these places:

home   school   neighborhood

Share with one another what you will do
there to build up God's kingdom this week.

Close by praying the Our Father together.

186

Talk with your teacher about ways you
and your family might use the "Faith
Alive" section. Ask your family to read
the parable of the mustard tree with
you. Try to pray the Our Father every
day with your family this week.

REVIEW ▪ TEST

Circle the letter beside the correct answer.

1. Jesus told parables to teach us how to
   a. plant seeds.
   b. live in God's kingdom.
   c. tell good stories.

2. The message of God's kingdom is
   a. only for Christians.
   b. only for adults.
   c. for everyone.

3. We help build up God's kingdom by
   a. living the Law of Love.
   b. making money.
   c. seeking power.

4. We are signs of God's kingdom when we
   a. make others listen to us.
   b. make money.
   c. make peace with others.

5. Write how you can be a sign of God's kingdom for someone this week.

   _____

   _____

FAITH ALIVE AT HOME AND IN THE PARISH

As Christians we must understand that the kingdom, or reign, of God is the power of God's life and love working in the world. By Baptism each of us is called to be a sign of God's reign by living our lives according to God's will—"God's will" is justice and peace, love and freedom, wholeness and fullness of life for all people, and the integrity of God's creation.

Planting a Seed

Have a family ceremony in which you plant a seed in your yard or in a jar or flowerpot. It may be a plant or flower seed. Let the growing plant be a symbol of your family's love and desire to put God first in your lives. As the seed grows, share with one another ways in which your family's love has grown. Talk about the way your love for one another helps to spread the message of God's kingdom and to build that kingdom, too.

Doing God's Will

Write these words on separate index cards: *peace, love, joy*. Make sure you have a card for each member of your family. Repeat the words as often as needed. Let each family member pick a card and tell what he or she will do to try to bring peace, love, or joy to your family. Then give one another a personal greeting of peace (hugs, kisses, etc.) or use the greeting of peace from the Mass.

Jesus, help us,
like You, to
carry our cross.

Our Life

Tim ran to the car to greet his grandmother.

"Happy day, Tim!" Granny said as she handed him a beautiful cake and a gift.

"It's not my birthday, Granny," said Tim.

"No, I know that. It's the day to celebrate your Baptism," explained Granny. "When I was a girl, we always celebrated our baptismal day every year with a little party. We also received a small religious gift. Open your present, Tim."

Tim unwrapped the box and found a beautiful cross on a chain. He put it on and hugged his grandmother.

"Let's cut the cake," she said.

Tell what you know about your Baptism.

Sharing Life

Talk together about the reasons why it is important for people to remember their Baptism.

What do you think the world would be like if each person tried to live as God's child?

Take a few minutes to think about the things we say that can bring either joy or sadness to others.

- How would you feel if you made a mistake in class and someone called you stupid?

- How would you feel if you wanted to play basketball and someone said, "You're no good. I don't want you on my team"?

What might a child of God say to you in each situation?

Now make a small cross. Use two sticks to form the cross. Ask a friend to help you tie the sticks together with purple yarn.

Put the cross near your bed to help you remember to think about the feelings of others before you speak.

In this lesson we will learn that Lent is a special time to try harder to live as a child of God.

We Will Learn

- Lent is the season of forty days before Easter. It begins on Ash Wednesday.

- During Lent we recall in a special way the great gift of God's grace we received in Baptism.

Our Catholic Faith

We Prepare for Easter

Lent, the forty days before Easter, is a very important season in the Church year. During Lent we think about the great gift of God's grace we first received in the sacrament of Baptism. The Church reminds us that as God's people we need to grow in God's grace, God's own life and love in us. We must also pray for those who are now preparing for Baptism at Easter time.

We begin Lent on Ash Wednesday by receiving ashes on our forehead. Ashes are a sign to others that we are sorry for our sins and want to try harder to live our Baptism by following Jesus.

During Lent we think about Jesus' great love in giving His life for us. We know that we have not always loved God and others as we should.

As God's people, we try to do better by being unselfish and by doing more loving things for others.

On Fridays during Lent, our parish may pray the stations of the cross. There are fourteen "stations," or stops, where we pause to remember Jesus' suffering. The stations tell the story of Jesus' passion (suffering) and death.

By Baptism we are united with Jesus in both His death and resurrection. If we are sorry for our sins and try to do better, we, too, will share in the joy of Jesus' resurrection. In this way we prepare to celebrate Easter.

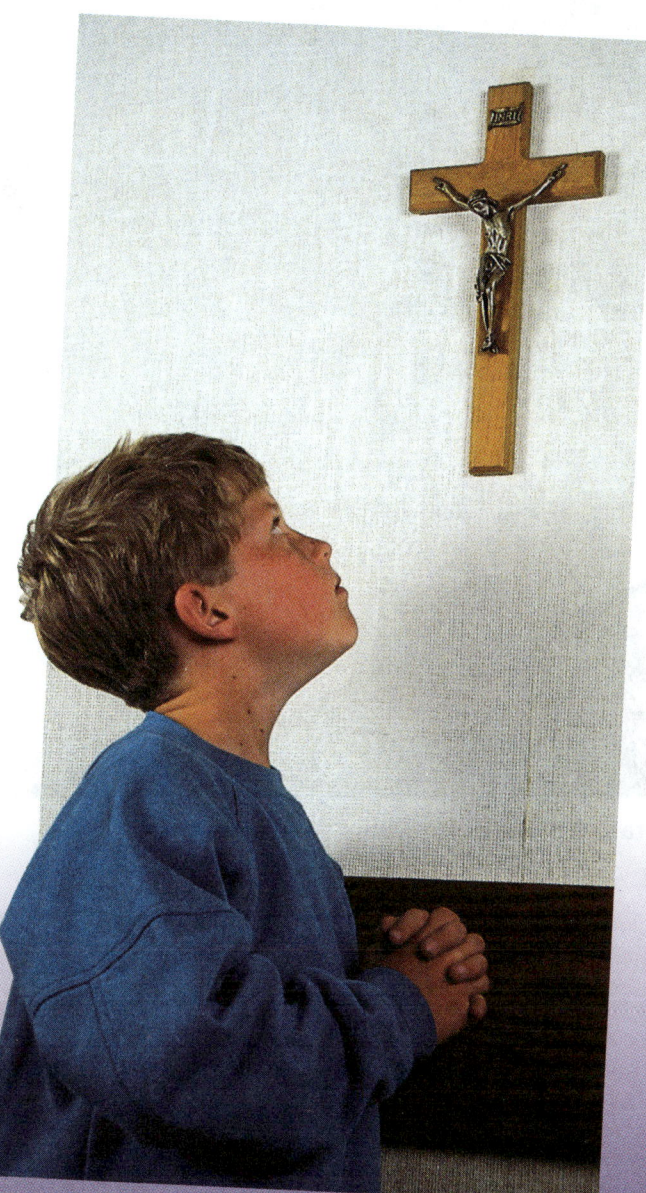

COMING TO FAITH

What loving things can you do this Lent to prepare for Easter?

Show what you remember about Lent.

1. Lent is a time to remember our

   _____ .

2. During Lent we pray for those who will

   be baptized at _____ .

3. The stations of the cross remind

   us of Jesus' _____

   and _____ .

PRACTICING FAITH

With your group, plan "living" stations of the cross. Show in a still scene what is happening in each station. Look at the scene, think quietly for a few moments, and then pray together in response.

✝ **A Lenten Prayer**

Leader: Jesus, You suffered and died to save us. Help us, this Lent, to follow You more closely, so we may come to know the joy of Your resurrection.

Reader 1: The first station: Jesus is condemned to death. (Pause)

All: Jesus, help me to be brave, to say and do what I believe.

Reader 2: The second station: Jesus takes up His cross. (Pause)

All: Jesus, help me to carry the small crosses of my life.

Reader 3: The third station: Jesus falls the first time. (Pause)

All: Jesus, help me do what is right, even when it is hard.

At the end of the stations, pray together:

All: We adore You, O Christ, and we bless You because by Your holy cross You have redeemed the world.

(Prepare prayers for stations 4–14.)

Station 6: Veronica wipes the face of Jesus.

192

Talk with your teacher about ways you and your family can use the "Faith Alive" section. Invite your family to pray together each day during Lent.

REVIEW · TEST

Complete the sentences below.

1. The season of Lent is the forty days before _____.

2. A special sign the Church uses to help us mark the beginning of Lent is

_____.

3. During Lent, the Church asks us to do _____.

4. The Stations of the Cross remind us of Jesus'

_____ and _____.

5. Tell one loving thing you can do during Lent to prepare for Easter. When can you do it?

_____

_____

_____

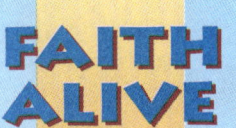

FAITH ALIVE AT HOME AND IN THE PARISH

This lesson helped to deepen your child's understanding of Lent. The focus is on our spiritual preparation for Easter, including recalling our Baptism, doing penance, and supporting those preparing for Baptism.

Lent helps us to take time to recall who we are as baptized Christians and what we need to do to deepen our commitment to Jesus Christ and His Church. We are called to a time of retreat and renewal in our Christian faith. It is an ideal time to deepen our commitment to the works of justice and mercy. We must also support by word and action those preparing for Baptism, Confirmation, and Eucharist at the Easter Vigil.

A Season to Reflect

If possible, set up a special place for your family to pray together during the season of Lent. You may want to display a cross or a picture of Jesus in your prayer place. You may also want to include photos and mementos of family baptismal celebrations.

Learn by heart **Faith Summary**

- Lent is the season of forty days before Easter. It begins on Ash Wednesday.

- During Lent we recall in a special way the gift of God's life we received in Baptism.

193

21 Easter

OUR LIFE

Who am I? Can you guess?
Write your answers.

I come from a seed.   _____

I come after winter.   _____

I come from a caterpillar.   _____

I come after rain.   _____

I come after sadness.   _____

I come after night.   _____

I come from a little egg.   _____

I come after death.   _____

Name other signs of new life.

SHARING LIFE

Tell a story about a special sign of new life that happened to you.

What new life does God want you to celebrate at Easter?

Why do we need signs of new life?

194

On a separate piece of paper, draw your favorite sign of new life. Be able to tell why it is your favorite. Then share it with your friends.

Now form small groups. Tape the new-life signs together in the shape of a cross as a reminder of your new life in Christ.

Hang up all the crosses. Gather around them and sing "Alleluia" to celebrate the new life Jesus won for us at Easter.

In this lesson we will learn more about our joyful celebration of Easter.

We Will Learn

- Easter is the celebration of the resurrection of Jesus.

- Jesus' resurrection is the promise of new life for all.

195

OUR CATHOLIC FAITH

We Celebrate Jesus' Resurrection

During Lent we follow Jesus through His last days. It is like the end of a cold winter. Then, finally, Easter comes like the new life of spring! Out of the sadness of Jesus' death comes the great joy of His resurrection. Jesus is alive!

In our parish church we find signs of new life and joy everywhere.

- We hear joyful music played.

- The choir and people sing Alleluia, Alleluia! Jesus Christ is risen today!

- The altar and other areas of the church are decorated with spring flowers.

- Priests and deacons wear white and gold vestments.

- The tall paschal candle stands beside the altar all during the Easter season. It reminds us that Jesus, the Light of the World, is risen.

- At Mass the priest or deacon reads the gospel story that tells why our sorrow has turned into joy. Jesus, our Savior, is risen! He has won new life for us! We share our joy with everyone.

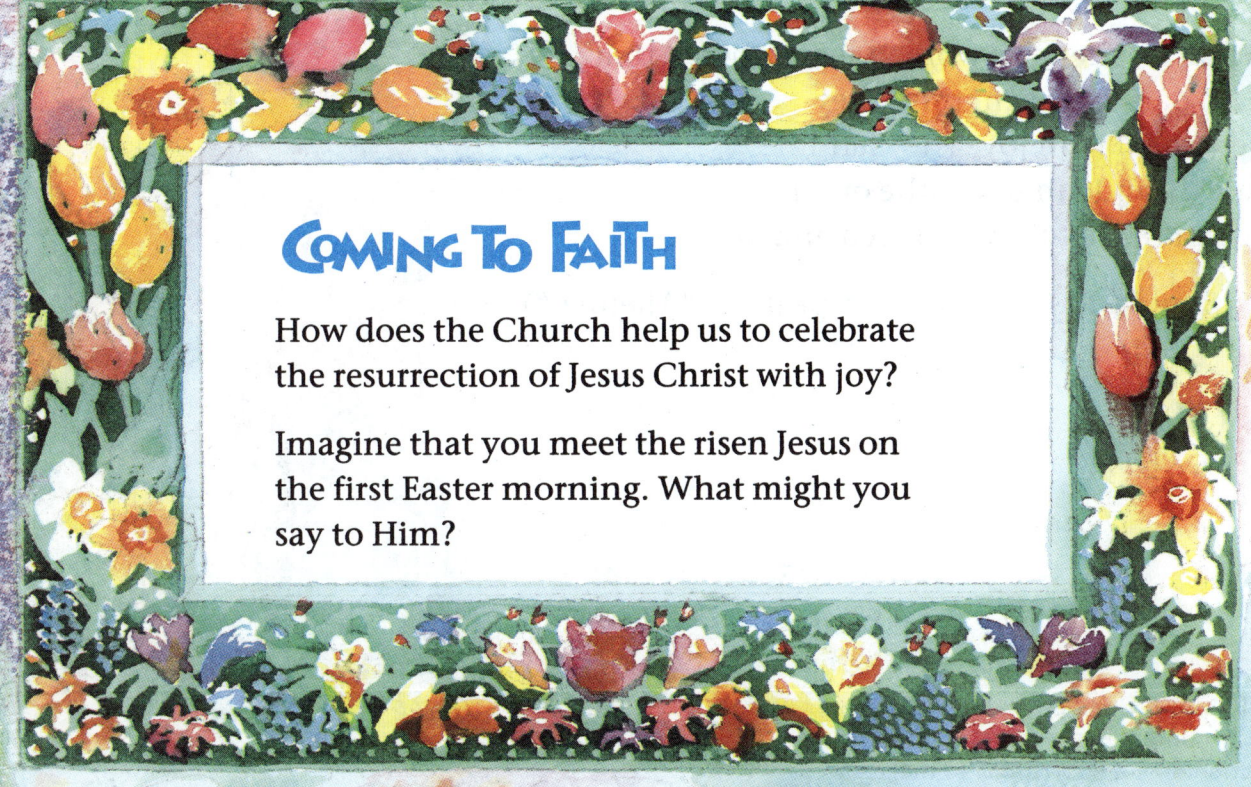

COMING TO FAITH

How does the Church help us to celebrate the resurrection of Jesus Christ with joy?

Imagine that you meet the risen Jesus on the first Easter morning. What might you say to Him?

PRACTICING FAITH

Celebrate Easter by acting out with your group the story of Jesus' resurrection. Begin by singing an Easter "Alleluia."

Reader 1: On the first day of the week at dawn, the women went to the tomb bringing spices to anoint Jesus' body. They found the stone rolled away, but when they went into the tomb, they did not find the body of Jesus.

Reader 2: While they stood there, two men in bright, shining garments appeared beside them. The women were very frightened.

Angel 1: Why do you search for the living one among the dead? Jesus is not here. He has been raised up.

Angel 2: Remember what Jesus told you— that He must be crucified, and on the third day rise again.

Reader 3: Then the women remembered that Jesus had told them this. They were filled with joy. They left quickly and ran to tell the other disciples what they had seen and heard.

All: (Sing an Easter hymn or repeat the "Alleluia.")

Talk with your teacher about ways you and your family can use the "Faith Alive" section. Invite your family to make an Easter poster or banner.

REVIEW • TEST

Put an **X** in the box next to each sentence that tells how the Church celebrates Jesus' resurrection at Easter.

1. ☐ We sing "Alleluia" in our parish churches.

2. ☐ At Mass we listen to the gospel story of Jesus' birth.

3. ☐ We celebrate the new life that Jesus has won for us.

4. ☐ We share our Easter joy with everyone around us.

5. Write your own Easter message here. With whom would you share it?

_____

_____

_____

FAITH ALIVE AT HOME AND IN THE PARISH

In this lesson your child reviewed the story and message of Easter. It is a story of joy and victory over death. In the risen Christ we place our hope for our own final resurrection to new life. Easter tells us that our sufferings, when joined with those of Jesus, can be overcome. It is this ultimate hope that Easter celebrates and that Christians give witness to in their lives.

Give Witness to the Resurrection

Make a family poster or banner to celebrate God's gift of new life. On it, print "Let us rejoice and be glad! Alleluia!" Invite family members to draw or paste pictures that show people and other living things for which they are grateful. Examples: the gift of Jesus, family and friends, the parish community, pets, flowers. Personal messages and poems might also be included. Display the poster or banner on the front door, in a window, or on a wall in your home.

Sing "Alleluia"

Ask your child to teach the family the Easter "Alleluia" he or she learned this week. If you wish, begin your Easter dinner celebration by joining hands around the table and singing the song together.

Learn by heart ### Faith Summary

- Easter is the celebration of the resurrection of Jesus.

- Jesus' resurrection is the promise of new life for all.

199

The Church Is One and Holy

Jesus, may we all be one in You.

OUR LIFE

Make a **Circle of Love** like this one.

1. On a sheet of paper, draw a circle the size of a quarter.

2. Now draw a much larger circle around the smaller one. Write your name on it. Then cut it out.

3. Write three friends' names on it. Join the names together with a line.

4. Fold your circle in half; then in half again. Cut out the small circle in the middle. Open your circle. Are you and your friends still "connected" by love?

Pretend that the hole you cut out of your circle is a small hurt. Should it separate you from those who love you?

Fold the circle again. How big a hole would you have to cut out before you break the Circle of Love?

How do you try to patch even a small "hole" in your Circle of Love?

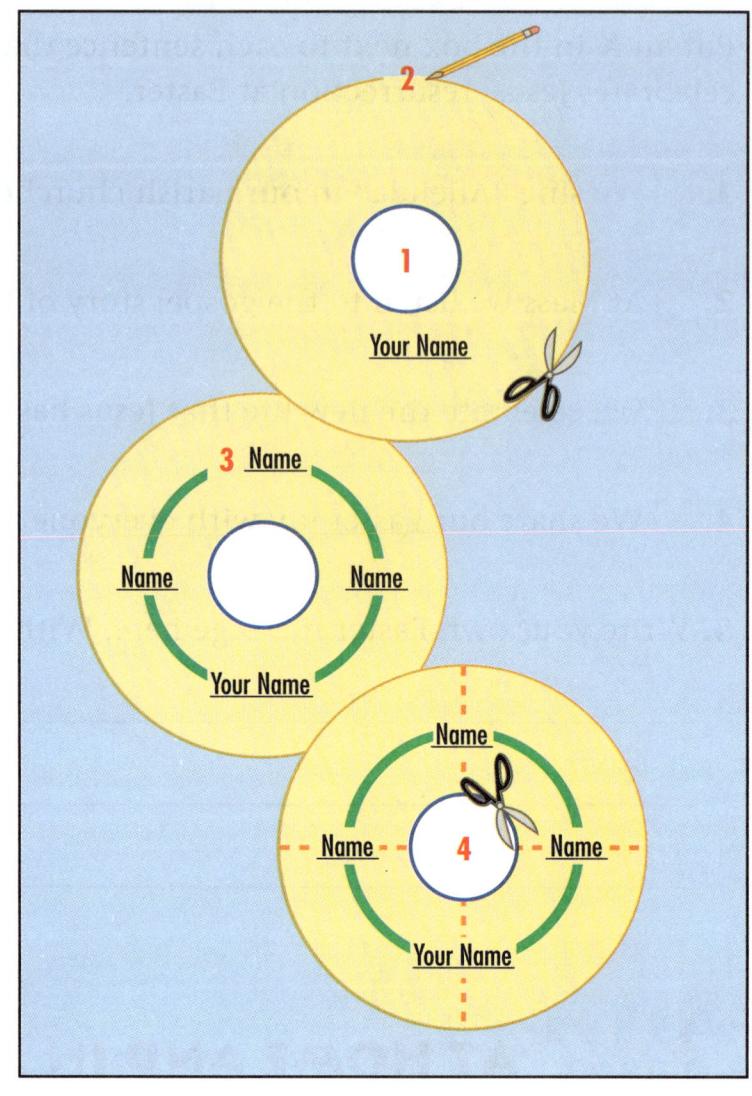

SHARING LIFE

How big a circle do you think Jesus wants for His friends?

Decide together how we can put everyone in the whole world on our Circle of Love.

Circle of Love

Join with a partner. Talk together about ways you might try to patch these small "holes" in your Circle of Love.

- A friend hurts your feelings. Later, that friend calls and says, "I'm sorry." You....

- You find out that a friend has lied to you. You....

- You have an argument with a friend at school. The next morning, you see that friend in class. You....

- You tell a lie that would hurt someone. You....

Share your ideas with your group.

Now decide: Why is it important to patch these "holes" in your Circle of Love?

In this lesson we will explore how we show others what it means to belong to Jesus' Church.

We Will Learn

- There are four marks of the Church.

- The first mark is that the Church is one.

- The second mark is that the Church is holy.

OUR CATHOLIC FAITH

■ Jesus, bless everyone in the Church.

■ How can people know that you are a friend of Jesus?

The Marks of the Church

People often wear uniforms, badges, or other identifying marks to show that they belong to a special group. As Christians, we want to show that we are growing as disciples of Jesus Christ.

We do not have a badge or a uniform to show others that we are Jesus' friends. But when people look at the way we live, they should see right away that we are Christians.

There are four great identifying marks in the Church that show people the kind of community that Jesus founded. We say that because of Jesus the Church is one, holy, catholic, and apostolic.

Catholics have been trying to live these marks since Jesus founded the Church. Sometimes we do well, other times we do not, but we must keep trying.

There are four **marks of the Church**:
one, holy, catholic, and apostolic.

The Marks of the Church		Symbol
One	Our Church is one in Jesus. We are united in one faith and love. We are to be signs of God's kingdom of love.	
Holy	Our Church is holy in Jesus. We are holy because we share in God's life. We try to live as Jesus did.	
Catholic	Our Church is catholic in Jesus. Jesus' message is for all people. Our community must invite everyone to belong, as Jesus did.	
Apostolic	Our Church is apostolic in Jesus. It shows it is faithful to the mission Jesus gave to the apostles. Our pope and bishops carry on the work of the apostles.	

Explain each mark of the Church.

How will you let others see one of these marks of the Church in your life?

OUR CATHOLIC FAITH

■ Jesus, help us to show the marks of the Church by the way we live.

■ Imagine some ways the friends of Jesus can show that they are one.

The Church Is One in Jesus

Jesus wants all His disciples everywhere to be united with Him and with one another in the Holy Spirit.

The first Christians were united by their faith and love in Jesus. They celebrated the Eucharist together and shared what they had with one another. They really lived and worked together as the Church, the body of Christ.

As time went on, the first Christians wrote down what they believed about God, about Jesus, and about the way Jesus wanted them to live. They wrote down the beliefs that united them.

Some of the early Christian writings became known as creeds. They tell what we believe about God and the Church.

One of the first creeds written is called the Apostles' Creed. Each time we say this creed, we proclaim our belief in the Blessed Trinity: God the Father, God the Son, and God the Holy Spirit. We show that as followers of Jesus, we are united in faith and love.

Saint Paul wrote about the beliefs that unite Christians. He said:

"There is one Lord, one faith, one Baptism. There is one God of all who works through all of us."
From Ephesians 4:5–6

We are made part of the one body of Christ through Baptism. As Catholics, we are united by the leadership of the pope and bishops. As Jesus' disciples, we are to show that we are one in faith and love with Him and one another.

- Explain how Jesus' disciples are united in the Church.

- Say the Apostles' Creed together now.

OUR CATHOLIC FAITH

■ Loving God, You are holy indeed.
Help us to live as Your holy people.

■ Tell about some ways you try to be holy.

The Church Is Holy in Jesus

Jesus called His disciples to live as holy people. The first Christians encouraged one another to lead holy lives. The Holy Spirit guided the Church to grow in holiness.

Growing in holiness means putting God first in our lives, even when it is hard. It means helping our Church to try always to put God first by living the way Jesus taught us.

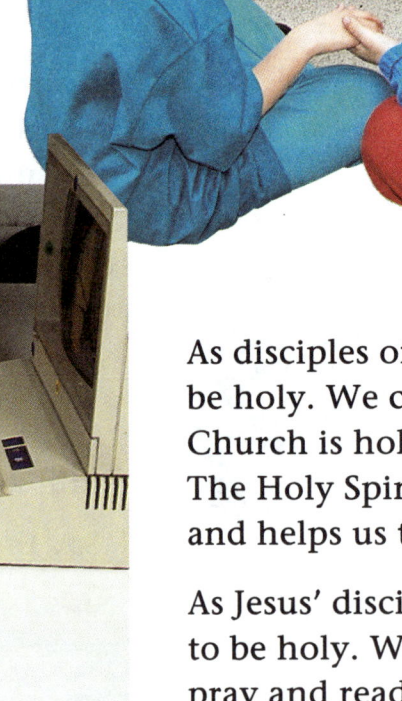

Learning together

As disciples of Jesus, all of us are called to be holy. We can show other people that the Church is holy by following Jesus' example. The Holy Spirit is present in the Church and helps us to lead holy lives.

As Jesus' disciples, we need to try always to be holy. We grow in holiness when we pray and read the Bible, celebrate the sacraments, and try our best to live as disciples of Jesus. We try to show in all we do that Jesus' Church is holy.

Growing in Holiness

One way we can grow in holiness is by turning to the advice and example of holy people.

Julian of Norwich was a holy woman whose writings have helped many people. She wrote down what she learned in prayer about God's great love for us. In her prayers, Julian often talked to God as both her Father and her Mother. This was her way of describing how loving and wonderful God is. Julian also taught that no matter how small and unimportant we may feel, God always loves us.

How do you feel about what Julian learned in prayer?

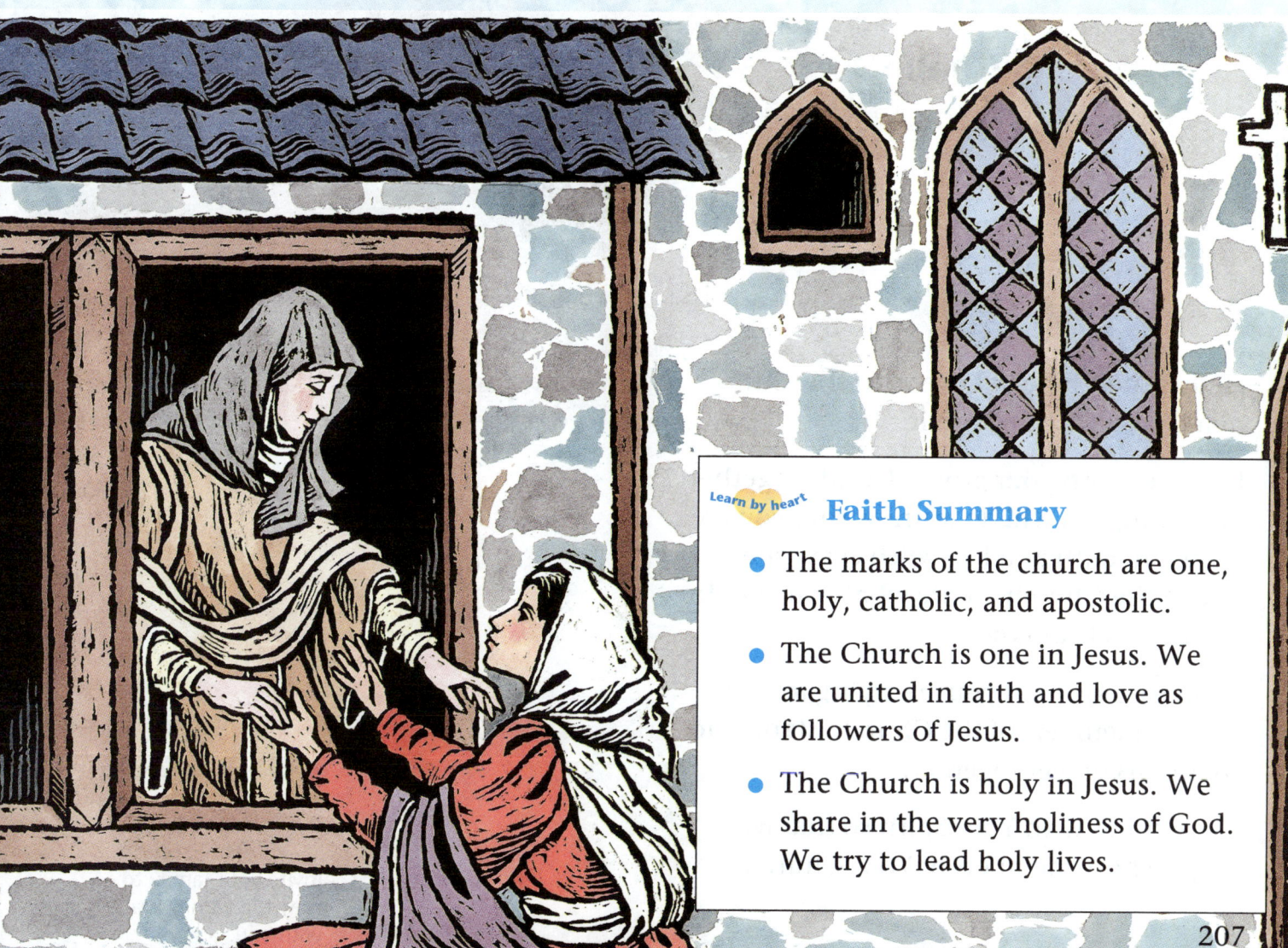

Learn by heart **Faith Summary**

- The marks of the church are one, holy, catholic, and apostolic.

- The Church is one in Jesus. We are united in faith and love as followers of Jesus.

- The Church is holy in Jesus. We share in the very holiness of God. We try to lead holy lives.

COMING TO FAITH

Name the four marks of the Church.
What does it mean to be one?

What does it mean to be holy?

Discuss together how you can become
holier people.

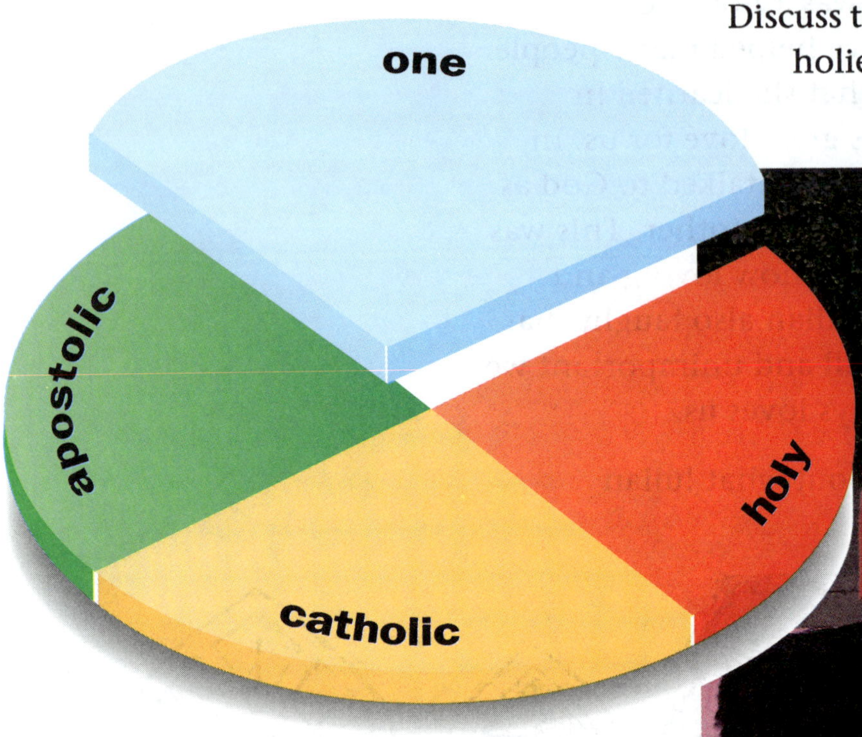

one

apostolic

holy

catholic

PRACTICING FAITH

Here is the Circle of Love with the four
marks of the Church on it.

Be "one" with your group. Decide together
one thing you will do to show that you are
united in faith and love with everyone
else in the Church. Write what you will do
on the Circle of Love.

Then to show that you are trying to grow
as holy members of the Church, stand and
share this prayer together.

✝ Jesus, fill us with Your Spirit so that we
may be holy members of Your Church.

Talk with your teacher
about ways you and your
family might use the
"Faith Alive" section.
Invite your family to
pray the Family Prayer
with you.

REVIEW · TEST

Answer.

1. Name the four marks of the Church.

_____

2. What does it mean to say the Church is one?

_____

3. How is the Church holy?

_____

4. How are people united in the Church?

_____

5. How can you become a holier person?

_____

_____

_____

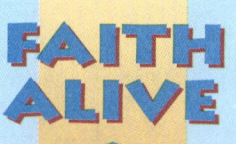

FAITH ALIVE AT HOME AND IN THE PARISH

In this lesson your child learned that the Church is recognized by four marks: one, holy, catholic, and apostolic. These marks of the Church challenge us to renew constantly our efforts to be the type of community of faith Jesus called us to be. Emphasis was placed on the first two marks, *one* and *holy*.

You Are the Church

The Second Vatican Council called the family "the domestic Church." Gather as a family to talk about the ways your family is a "little Church," a community of Jesus' friends living the Law of Love. Ask Jesus to bless your home and your family.

† Family Prayer

Here is a prayer to praise God for calling you to unity and holiness, both as a family and as members of the larger Church community.

Leader: O God, we praise You and thank You for bringing us together as a community.

All: All life and holiness come from God.

Leader: O God, we praise You and thank You for sharing with us the gift of Your life.

All: All life and holiness come from God.

Leader: O God, we praise You and thank You for making us one in faith and love.

All: All life and holiness come from God.

Leader: O God, we praise You and thank You for calling us to be holy.

All: All life and holiness come from God.

Leader: O God, we praise You and thank You for the gift of Your Holy Spirit.

All: All life and holiness come from God.

Dear God, we are all Your children. Teach us to respect and love one another.

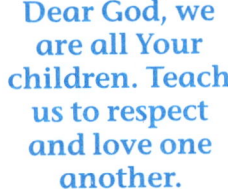

Our Life

Look at these pictures.
Do you think these children could be Catholic? Why or why not?

Are there Catholics who:
- dress differently from you?
- eat different foods?
- speak a different language?
- enjoy different music?
- celebrate different holidays?

What are some things that all Catholics share in common?

Sharing Life

Why do we have so many different kinds of people in the Catholic Church?

Why are they all welcome?
Share together: is the Church for everyone?

Imagine you are on a journey in space. You land on a distant planet. To your surprise, you land in front of a building called Friends of the Universe.

A robot greets you and says, "The Friends of the Universe welcome you. You may join our friendly community if your skin is purple and you have lots of money."

Would you be accepted by this community? How would you feel?

Discuss with a partner whether the Friends of the Universe is really a friendly community. What should the robot have said? Share your ideas with the group.

Now decide: How does the Catholic Church show others that it is a friendly community?

In this lesson we will learn more about ways we show others that Jesus' Church welcomes everyone.

We Will Learn

- The third mark of the Church is that it is catholic.

- The fourth mark of the Church is that it is apostolic.

- Catholics should try to live the four marks of the Church.

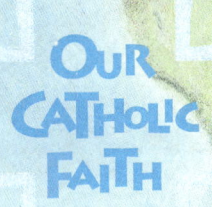

Jesus, we praise You and thank You for welcoming all people into Your Church.

How does your parish make people feel welcome?

The Church Is Catholic in Jesus

Jesus welcomed everyone into His community of disciples. He taught His community to welcome everyone, too. His good news was for everyone.

Jesus' disciples bring the good news of God's love everywhere. Today the Church is all over the world. It is on every continent and in every country.

Being catholic is the third mark of the Church. Catholic means that we welcome all and proclaim the message of Jesus to all. The Church welcomes and has good news for all people.

Our parish is truly catholic when all people feel welcome, no matter what their language, color, or race may be. When the poor and the rich, the sick and the healthy, the young and the old all feel welcome, then our parish shows it is truly catholic.

Our parish community can have different kinds of celebrations. At Christmas, for example, we might celebrate with Spanish, African, German, or Chinese customs, depending on who belongs to our parish. Respecting everyone's customs is one way we show that the Church welcomes all people.

Catholic means that the Church welcomes all people and has a message for all people.

Saint Elizabeth Ann Seton

Here is the story of a woman who shared the message of Jesus with children in our own country.

Elizabeth Ann Seton came from a wealthy Protestant family. She married and had five children. After her husband's death, she became a Catholic. Besides caring for her own children, Elizabeth had great concern for all young people, especially the poor. She founded the first parish school in our country to educate children and help them grow in their Catholic faith.

Elizabeth Ann Seton was the first American-born citizen to be canonized a saint. We celebrate her feast day on January 4.

Write a prayer to Saint Elizabeth Ann Seton. Ask her to help you grow in your Catholic faith, as she did.

Saint Elizabeth Ann Seton

Explain what the word *catholic* means.

How will you help to make people who are different from you feel welcome in your parish?

OUR CATHOLIC FAITH

Pope John Paul II greeting Native Americans

- Lord Jesus, open our hearts to welcome all people as you do.

- What is the mission Jesus gives you as His disciple?

The Church Is Apostolic in Jesus

Jesus asked the apostle Peter to be the first leader and guide of His Church. Jesus said, "Peter, you are a rock, and on this rock foundation I will build My church."
From Matthew 16:18

Together with the other apostles, Peter was to make sure that the teachings of Jesus were passed on. Peter was to lead the first disciples in carrying on Jesus' mission, or work.

In time, the leaders who continued the work of the apostles were called bishops. The bishop of Rome, Peter's successor, came to be called the pope, the leader of the whole Catholic Church.

Today the pope and bishops lead us in carrying on the mission of Jesus.

- They teach us the good news of Jesus and the truths of the Catholic faith.

- They celebrate Mass and the sacraments with us.

- They help us to live as a community, united in faith and love.

- They lead us in serving the poor and working for justice and peace.

From time to time, our bishops gather in Rome with our Holy Father, the pope. They advise the pope on important matters and challenges that the Church faces in the modern world.

The Holy Spirit is always with our pope and bishops to guide them. We pray for them to lead us well in carrying on the mission of Jesus.

The Church shows it is apostolic by being faithful to the mission Jesus gave to the apostles. We say that the Church is apostolic in Jesus. As Catholics, we are all called to be faithful to Jesus' saving mission to spread the good news and bring about God's kingdom.

How does the Church show that it is apostolic?

How will you help our pope and bishops to carry on the work of the apostles?

Holy Spirit, guide our pope and bishops as they lead us in living the Catholic faith.

How can others know that you are a Catholic Christian?

Living the Four Marks

As disciples of Jesus, each of us must show the Church's four marks to others. We do this when we live our Catholic faith.

When we live our creed and Jesus' great commandment of love, we show that the Church is one. When we put God first in our lives and receive the sacraments, we show that the Church is holy.

Every time we make someone feel welcome in our parish, we show that the Church is catholic. When we help carry on Jesus' mission and live and share His good news, we show that the Church is apostolic.

Honoring Saint Peter

Saint Peter, the leader of the apostles, was crucified on a hill outside of the city of Rome. The disciples buried him there. Year after year, Christians came to pray at the tomb of Saint Peter. To honor him, a small church was built over the tomb. Many years later a great new church was built there. Today we call that church Saint Peter's Basilica.

The great basilica has been a place of prayer for Catholics from all over the world. They come to pray at the tomb of Saint Peter. They come to be reminded that we are all one in Jesus Christ and in the Church that He founded.

Dear Saint Peter,
Jesus chose you to be the leader of the apostles. Pray for the Church that we might truly be one, holy, catholic, and apostolic.

Learn by heart **Faith Summary**

- The Church is catholic in Jesus. It welcomes all, has a message for all, and is all over the world.

- The Church is apostolic in Jesus. It is founded on the apostles and carries on the mission Jesus gave them.

- All Catholics try to live the four marks of the Church: one, holy, catholic, and apostolic.

COMING TO FAITH

Explain the mark of the Church that means the Church welcomes and has good news for people everywhere.

Explain the mark of the Church that means the Church is faithful to the mission Jesus gave the apostles.

Who takes Peter's place today in leading the whole Catholic Church?

Decide together what your group can do to help the Church be more catholic and apostolic.

PRACTICING FAITH

With a few group members, invite someone else to Mass as a sign that our Church is catholic. We welcome all and have the message of Jesus' good news for all.

† During Mass say this prayer: Loving God, help our pope and bishops carry on the work of the apostles.

Talk with your teacher about ways you and your family might use the "Faith Alive" section. Ask a family member to go over the *Faith Summary* with you before you do the *Review Test*. Invite your family to pray for the leaders of the Church.

REVIEW ■ TEST

Circle the letter beside the correct answer.

1. Jesus' disciples brought good news to the
   a. poor and sick only.
   b. whole world.
   c. rich and healthy only.

2. Catholic means
   a. holy.
   b. for all people.
   c. just.

3. The apostle Jesus asked to be the first leader of His Church was
   a. Peter.
   b. Paul.
   c. John.

4. Apostolic means
   a. carrying on the mission Jesus gave to the apostles.
   b. being one of the twelve apostles.
   c. going back to the Old Testament.

5. How can you help the Church bring Jesus' message to others?

   _____

   _____

FAITH ALIVE AT HOME AND IN THE PARISH

In this lesson your child learned about the other two marks of the Church, *catholic* and *apostolic*. Ask your child to tell you what each means and how we can show these marks in our daily lives.

Sharing Jesus' Good News

Help your child to appreciate that since the time of the apostles, many men and women have continued to bring Jesus' good news to everyone. Read with your child the story of Saint Elizabeth Ann Seton on page 213. Then talk about the people in your school who help your child learn to live Jesus' good news. Conclude by praying together the prayer your child wrote to Saint Elizabeth Ann.

Praying for Church leaders

Encourage your family to pray that the leaders of the Church may be faithful to the mission of the apostles. If possible, have your family look through magazines and/or newspapers for a picture of the Holy Father and of your local bishop. Mount the pictures on construction paper to make a poster. Write the name of the pope and of the bishop under the appropriate picture.

Display the poster where your family will see it. Each time family members pass the poster, encourage them to pray that the Holy Spirit will guide the pope and the bishop in their daily tasks of leading and serving the Church.

24 We Are All God's People

Dear God, help
us to live in
peace with all
people.

Muslims

What are each of these peoples
saying about God?

Tell something you do to worship God.

Sharing Life

Talk over together how you think
Jesus wants us to act toward people
who worship God differently from us.

Our Life

Every day Hassan and his father listen
as the daily call to prayer is sounded.
They hear the *Shahadah* proclaimed
from the highest tower of the mosque:
"There is no God but God; Muhammad
is the prophet of God." Hassan and his
father join the other men at the
mosque. They bow in prayer facing
Mecca, the holy city of Islam.

The Navajo use special songs and
chants called the *Blessingway*. The
chants are sometimes sung to cure the
sick and sometimes to ensure the well-
being of the whole community. The
chants tell stories about how the
Navajo came to the earth at creation
from the Great Spirit.

Navajo sandpainting

Read these "what if" questions. Tell how you think Jesus would answer each one.

- What if someone said, "Only Catholics can get to heaven"?

- What if some children made fun of a Jewish man who was wearing a yarmulke on his head?

Make up a few more "what if" questions about people who worship God differently from us. Share them with your group. After each question, ask, "What would Jesus answer?"

In this lesson we will learn more about people who worship differently from us.

The Jewish Feast of Succoth

Burmese woman at prayer

The Dalai Lama

We Will Learn

- Through the Jewish people, we received our belief in the one true God.

- All Christians are our sisters and brothers in Christ.

- We work for unity among all Christians.

221

Our Catholic Faith

- God, help us to respect all people.
- Does God love all people? Why or why not?

We Are All God's People

God is the loving creator of everyone in our human family. People all over the world, Christians and people of other religions, worship God in different ways. God wants us to love and respect them all, as God does.

We Christians have a special bond with our Jewish brothers and sisters. The Jews are called the chosen people. They were chosen to tell the whole world that there is only one true God. With the Jews, Christians treasure the Ten Commandments.

Every Catholic is a Christian. As Christians we respect the Jewish religion in a special way. Through the Jewish people we received our belief in one God. Through them we also received the Ten Commandments.

Jesus was born into a Jewish family. The Holy Family worshiped God and celebrated the same feasts that our Jewish friends celebrate today.

When we worship God, we should pray for the Jewish people, who taught us about the one God. We should respect the way Jewish people worship God.

Finish coloring this prayer that both Christians and Jews pray.

HEAR, O ISRAEL! THE LORD OUR GOD IS ONE.

Why do Christians owe Jews special honor and respect?

How will you show the world that you believe in the one true God?

OUR CATHOLIC FAITH

■ O God, bless all people who believe in You.

■ Do you know any Christians who are not Catholics? Tell about them. Why should we respect them?

Our Christian Sisters and Brothers

Jesus wanted all His disciples to be united as one community. But as the Church grew, different members began to disagree about what Jesus wanted the Church to be like. Some decided not to remain a part of the Catholic Church.

Today there are many kinds of Christians who are not Catholic Christians. But because they are baptized, they also are members of the body of Christ. By Baptism, they are our sisters and brothers in Christ. We pray that God will unite us all again.

There are Christians who are called Orthodox Christians. Their leaders and our pope have met and prayed that one day there will be unity again between our two Churches.

Many Christians belong to Protestant churches. Some of these are the Episcopal, Lutheran, Presbyterian, Methodist, and Baptist churches. Together we are all brothers and sisters in Christ.

Praying in a Russian Orthodox church

A **Rite** is a part of the Catholic Church that has its own liturgy, laws, and customs.

The Catholic Church is our home in God's family. In the Catholic Church we have a number of different groups. Most Catholics follow the Roman (or Latin) Rite; others follow one of the Eastern Rites. No matter which Rite we belong to, all Catholics are united under the leadership of the pope.

All Catholics celebrate the same seven sacraments. We know and believe the same creed. We have a special love for Mary, whom we honor as the mother of Jesus.

Jesus wants all Christians to be united in one Church. He wants us to respect and love all our brothers and sisters in Christ. On the night before He died, Jesus prayed for His disciples, "May they all be one."
From John 17:21

Today, many Christians are working together to bring about this unity in the body of Christ.

Eastern Rite wedding ceremony

■ What would you say if someone asked whether you are proud to be Catholic?

■ How will you show respect for other Christian faiths?

225

OUR CATHOLIC FAITH

- Jesus, we pray that all Christians may be one.

- What do you think unity among Christians means?

Unity in Our Christian Community

The Catholic Church today proclaims the message of Jesus everywhere. The Church tries to bring the peace of Jesus Christ to people all over the world. When we are fair to others in our family and in our parish, we build up God's kingdom.

There is good news today. Many people are working hard to bring all Christian churches together again. This work is called the ecumenical movement.

We can help to bring all Christians together by:

- praying Jesus' prayer for unity each day;

- learning about and respecting the ways in which other Christians worship God.

Only if we respect and love one another can we hope that all Christians will be united again.

A Catholic priest with the former Archbishop of Canterbury, England (Anglican)

Rites in the Catholic Church

Within the Catholic Church we have different Rites. We have the Latin (or Roman) Rite and many Eastern Rites. No matter which Rite we belong to, all Catholics are united in the one Catholic Church. We share the same creed, the same seven sacraments, and the same leader, the pope.

As Catholics we celebrate the same faith differently from Rite to Rite. Here are some examples.

- Latin Rite Catholics usually genuflect before the Blessed Sacrament. Eastern Rite Catholics bow deeply.

- Latin Rite Catholics have Mass prayers and hymns that are different from those used by Eastern Rite Catholics. But we all share the same Eucharist.

- In the Latin Rite, priests wear vestments that look different from those worn in the Eastern Rites.

Would you like to know more about Eastern Rite Catholic churches? Maybe you could visit one in your area.

An icon of Our Lady

Receiving Communion in the Eastern Rite

Learn by heart

Faith Summary

- Through the Jewish people, we received our belief in the one true God.

- All Christians are our sisters and brothers in Jesus Christ.

- The Catholic Church works for unity among all Christians.

227

COMING TO FAITH

How can you learn more about the different churches or other places of worship in your neighborhood?

Here's an idea. Maybe your teacher could help you arrange a visit to a synagogue or Protestant church.

You could take notes and discuss what is the same and what is different about these other houses of prayer.

PRACTICING FAITH

Together imagine how you and your friends will work for unity among all Christians and respect for people of all religions.

Perhaps you could discover whether there is a third-grade group in a local Protestant church. Invite them to share fun and prayer with you.

† Now gather as a group in a prayer circle. Close your eyes and listen again as one person reads Jesus' prayer from page 225. After a few moments of quiet, end by saying, "Holy Spirit, help us to live at peace with all people."

Talk with your teacher about ways you and your family might use the "Faith Alive" section. Share with your family how different people worship God. Talk with them about ways your parish works for Christian unity.

228

REVIEW · TEST

Circle **T** for **True** or **F** for **False.**
If you are not sure, circle **?**.

1. All Catholics follow the same Rite. **T** **F** **?**

2. Jesus was born into a Jewish family. **T** **F** **?**

3. All Christians are our brothers and sisters
   in Jesus Christ. **T** **F** **?**

4. The Catholic Church discourages unity
   among all Christian groups. **T** **F** **?**

5. What would you do to show that you respect people of
   different religions?

   _____

   _____

   _____

FAITH ALIVE AT HOME AND IN THE PARISH

In this lesson your child learned that God's love is universal. As Catholics we must respect the right that other people have to worship God in their own ways. Our conviction concerning God's love for all people demands that we give them such respect. This respect does not diminish the great treasure, the uniqueness of truth we have in the Catholic Church. Your child has also been asked to pray and work for unity among the Christian churches as encouraged by the Church's teaching on ecumenism. Discuss ways your family can help this movement by:

■ learning about and respecting the ways in which other Christians worship God;

■ praying daily for Christian unity.

Working for Christian Unity

Talk with your family about what your parish is doing to bring Christian churches closer together. Plan what you can do to support your parish's efforts in this regard.

Respecting the Jewish People

Share how important it is to respect our Jewish brothers and sisters, from whom we received our belief in the one true God. If there is a Jewish synagogue in your neighborhood, try to learn more about the way its members worship God. Remember that anti-Semitism is a sin and has no place in a Catholic's life.

Holy Mary,
Mother of God,
pray for us.

Our Life

In 1521 a beautiful lady appeared to Juan Diego, a poor Aztec Indian in Mexico. It was Mary, the mother of Jesus. She asked Juan to tell the Mexican people how much she and her son, Jesus, loved them. Juan ran and told the bishop what had happened, but the bishop asked for a sign.

Juan returned to the place where Mary had appeared. There he found roses blooming in the cold winter air. He gathered them in his cloak and ran back to the bishop.

As Juan unfolded his cloak, the roses fell out. But there, on his cloak, the bishop saw a picture of the beautiful lady Juan had seen! We call her Our Lady of Guadalupe.

Imagine Mary appearing to you as she did to Juan Diego. What might she ask you to do?

Sharing Life

With your friends, act out the story of Our Lady of Guadalupe.

Then share what you already know about Mary, the Mother of God.

Work in groups of three.

1. Have one group member draw an eight-inch circle.

2. Cut the circle in four equal pieces.

3. Give one piece to each group member. Set aside the fourth piece.

Imagine that each of the three pieces is part of the cloak Juan wore in the story. On each piece, write one thing you know and love about Mary. Then decorate each piece with a border.

Now work together to make up a short prayer to Mary. Ask one group member to write your prayer on the fourth piece.

Paste the pieces back together on a sheet of paper. Share your cloak with your classmates.

Display all the cloaks to show that you honor Mary, the Mother of God.

In this lesson we will learn more about Mary and why we honor her in a special way.

☀️We Will Learn

- Mary is the Mother of all Christians.
- Catholics honor Mary on her feast days.
- We often ask Mary to pray for us.

OUR CATHOLIC FAITH

■ Holy Mary, Mother of God, pray for us.

■ Share some of your own feelings about Mary.

Mary Our Mother

Catholics give special honor to the Blessed Virgin Mary, the mother of Jesus. The stories we know about Mary were handed down to us by the first Christians.

Mary learned from her family to love God with all her heart. She always tried to do God's will.

Mary was chosen to be the mother of Jesus, the Son of God. Because of this, God gave Mary the privilege of being free of original sin, the first sin of the human race that affects all people. We call this privilege Mary's immaculate conception.

When God asked Mary to be the mother of Jesus, our Savior, she could have refused. Instead, Mary said yes to God. She knew it would be hard, but she trusted that God would help her.

Mary and Joseph taught Jesus all about the Jewish religion. From them, Jesus learned how to pray and to care for the poor and needy.

The **immaculate conception** is Mary's privilege of being free from original sin from the first moment of her life.

When Jesus left home to begin His great mission, Mary sometimes went to hear Him preach the good news of God's love.

Mary was with Jesus when He was put to death on the cross. From His cross, Jesus looked down with great love at His mother, Mary, and at His disciple John. Jesus said to Mary, "Here is your son," and to John He said, "Here is your mother."
From John 19:26, 27

From that moment Mary became the mother of all Jesus' disciples. She is our mother now, too.

After Jesus ascended to heaven, Mary comforted the early Christians.

At the end of her life Mary, the Mother of God, was taken, body and soul, into heaven to be happy with God forever.

We call this the assumption of Mary into heaven.

Mary still comforts and prays for us today. We love Mary as our mother and the Mother of the Church.

- Explain how Mary is a mother to all of Jesus' followers today.

- How will you show love for Mary your mother?

233

■ Pray the Hail Holy Queen.
(See page 278.)

■ When do you ask Mary to pray
for you? What do you say?

Mary's Feast Days

All over the world, Catholics honor
Mary with wonderful celebrations. Here
are some of Mary's feasts.

December 8—Immaculate Conception

We celebrate God's special blessing to
Mary of being born free from original
sin. We ask Mary to help us try each day
to be better disciples of her son, Jesus.

December 12—Our Lady of Guadalupe

On this day we remember and celebrate
the love our Blessed Mother has for the
poor people of Mexico. We ask Mary to
pray for us that we may love and be fair
to everyone.

January 1—Mary, Mother of God

On New Year's Day, we begin the year
by celebrating that Mary is Jesus'
mother and our mother, too. We ask
Mary to help us love God and others,
as she did.

March 25—The Annunciation

We celebrate Mary's yes when God asked her to be the mother of Jesus, our Savior. We ask Mary to pray for us when we have hard choices to make.

May 31—The Visitation

We celebrate the long journey that Mary made to visit her elderly cousin Elizabeth, who was going to have a baby. We ask Mary to help us respect all life, especially the lives of babies waiting to be born.

August 15—The Assumption

We know that Mary is in heaven with God. We ask Mary to help us follow the way of Jesus, her son.

September 8—The Birth of Mary

We celebrate God's gift of Mary to us. We ask her to pray for us that we may love God and live as Mary did.

Circle your favorite feast day. What special thing will you do to honor Mary on this day?

_____

_____

_____

_____

_____

- Take turns explaining the feast days of Mary to one another.

- What prayer do you want to say to Mary now?

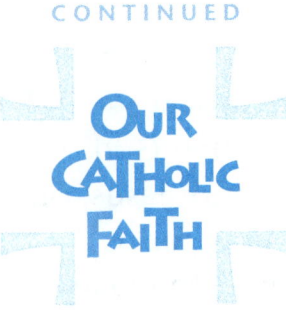

OUR
CATHOLIC
FAITH

Catholics also pray the rosary to honor Mary. We use prayer beads called rosary beads to help us count the Hail Marys, Our Fathers, and other prayers we say in the rosary.

There are five decades in a rosary. Each decade has eleven beads: one for the Our Father and ten for the Hail Marys.

While we pray the decades of the rosary, we think of the happy or sad times in the lives of Mary and Jesus. We call these the mysteries of the rosary. (See page 278.)

▪ Pray the Hail Mary together.

▪ What prayers to Mary do you know by heart? When do you say them?

Prayers to Mary

Catholics have many beautiful prayers to Mary. The Hail Mary is her special prayer. We pray some of the same words Mary heard when she was asked to be the Mother of God.

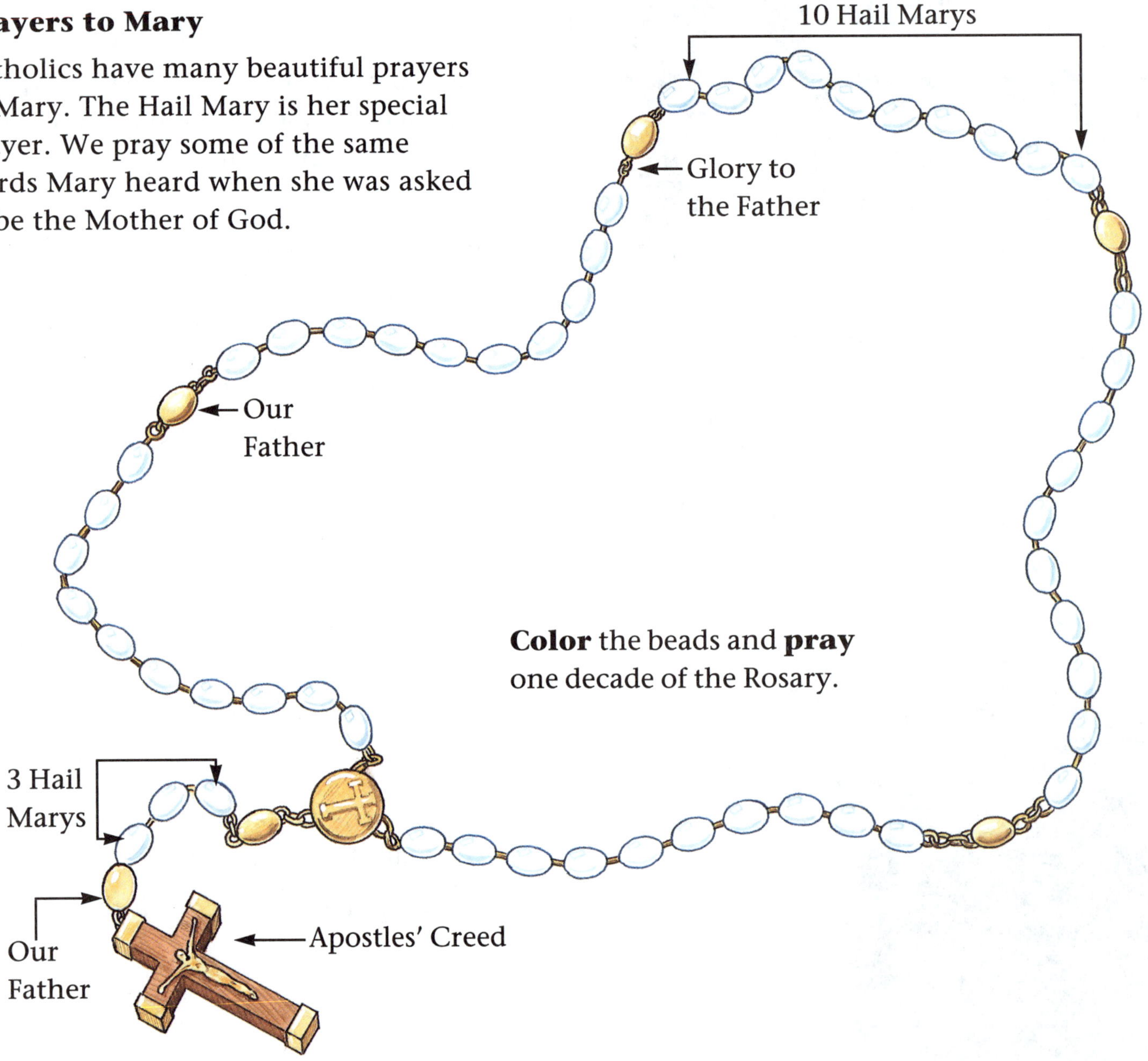

10 Hail Marys

←Glory to the Father

←Our Father

Color the beads and **pray** one decade of the Rosary.

3 Hail Marys

Our Father

←Apostles' Creed

Our Lady of Lourdes

Each year millions of people travel to the small town of Lourdes in France. They do this because they believe the Blessed Virgin Mary appeared there to a young girl. The girl's name was Bernadette.

Mary asked that a church be built at Lourdes, where people could come to pray.

Today many people go to Lourdes to pray for cures from sickness and disease. But many more people go there because it is a special place to honor Mary.

Every day crowds gather there to ask Mary to pray for them to her son, Jesus. We celebrate the feast of Our Lady of Lourdes on February 11.

What prayer do you want to say to Our Lady of Lourdes now?

Learn by heart **Faith Summary**

- Mary, Mother of God, is our mother, too.
- Mary is the Mother of the Church.
- Catholics have a special devotion to Mary.

Coming to Faith

How do you feel knowing that Mary is your mother in heaven?

Make an "Honor Mary" booklet. Use one page for each feast day. Print the name of the feast day. Draw or paste a picture of what we celebrate about Mary on that day. Then write your own prayer to Mary for that feast.

Plan the first page of your booklet here.

Prayer _____

_____

_____

_____

Practicing Faith

† Gather together around a statue or picture of Mary. Play quiet music in the background. Choose those who will take each line of the litany. All respond, "Pray for us."

Mary, Mother of God,	pray for us.
Mary, free from all sin,	pray for us.
Mary, always faithful,	pray for us.
Mary, Mother of the Church,	pray for us.
Mary, our mother,	pray for us.
Hail Mary	

Talk with your teacher about ways you and your family might use the "Faith Alive" section. Invite your family to share how they feel about Mary, the mother of Jesus and our mother, too.

REVIEW ▪ TEST

Match each feast of Mary with its meaning.

1. Immaculate Conception

___ Mary visited her cousin Elizabeth.

2. Mary, the Mother of God

___ Mary was taken, body and soul, into heaven.

3. The Annunciation

___ Mary is Jesus' mother and our mother, too.

4. The Assumption

___ Mary said yes when God asked her to be the mother of Jesus.

___ Mary was free from original sin from the first moment of her life.

5. Tell how you feel about having Mary as your mother.

_____

_____

_____

FAITH ALIVE AT HOME AND IN THE PARISH

In this lesson your child learned why the Blessed Virgin Mary is so special to Catholics. Your child needs to learn true devotion to Mary from you and your family. He or she needs to learn from you how important Mary is to our Catholic spirituality. We honor Mary as the Mother of God and as our mother, too. We also regard her as the first and foremost disciple of Jesus, because through her the Word became flesh.

Honoring Mary as Mother

Talk with your family about the important part Mary played in the Holy Family. Encourage family members to share their feelings about Mary as a loving mother. Then say a prayer or sing a hymn to Mary together. Ask Mary, the mother of Jesus and our mother, to pray for your family and families all over the world.

Reading about Mary

Purchase or borrow from the library a children's book that tells the story of Our Lady of Guadalupe. Take a few minutes each evening to read a portion of the story with your child. Talk about the story and the illustrations. Then, in your own words, ask Mary to pray for you and invite your child to do the same. Conclude by asking Mary to pray to her son, Jesus, for all people.

Jesus, help us to be Your peacemakers.

Our Life

Our Church is more than just a place
For praying silent prayer—
It's people helping people
With love and constant care.

For worship, help, and serving,
Our parish shows the way—
To share the work of Jesus
Each and every day.

Name some of the people in your parish who do the work of Jesus. Don't forget yourself!

Sharing Life

Tell what you and your friends have done this year to show

• you love God and others.
• you are peacemakers.

Why is it sometimes difficult to be a peacemaker?

How will you try to keep growing in your faith?

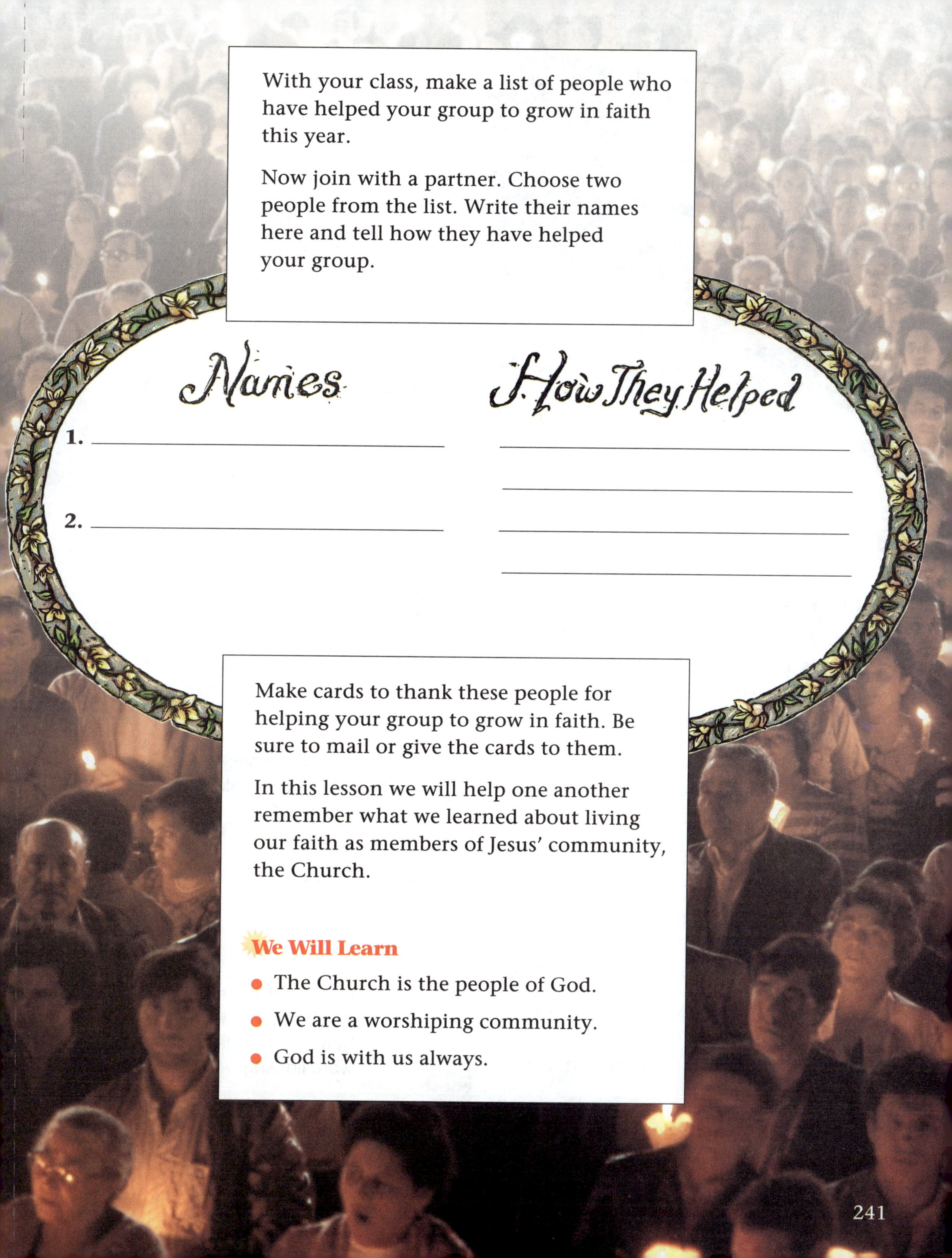

With your class, make a list of people who have helped your group to grow in faith this year.

Now join with a partner. Choose two people from the list. Write their names here and tell how they have helped your group.

Names

How They Helped

1. _____ _____

_____

2. _____ _____

_____

Make cards to thank these people for helping your group to grow in faith. Be sure to mail or give the cards to them.

In this lesson we will help one another remember what we learned about living our faith as members of Jesus' community, the Church.

We Will Learn

- The Church is the people of God.
- We are a worshiping community.
- God is with us always.

Welcome

- God, bless our Church community.
- How can you be an active member of your parish community?

Move 3 spaces ahead. You received Jesus in Holy Communion.

Move 2 spaces back. You were unfair to a friend.

Move ahead 2 spaces. You helped make peace between friends who were fighting.

The Church, the People of God

We have learned that the Church is God's own people. It is a worshiping and caring community. We all have a part to play in building up this community and in bringing Jesus' good news of God's kingdom, or reign, to others.

The game **"Who's Who?"** will help you remember some ways people do this.

1. Cut out 13 strips of paper. Copy on each strip the name of a person from the chart.

2. On the other side of the strip write what that person does. Place the strips in a box.

3. Choose a partner. Take turns drawing a strip. Read the person's name and ask your partner to tell what that person does to help build up the Church.

4. Use markers and move up a space on the game board for each correct answer.

Who's Who?

Name of Person	What Person Does
pope	the leader of the whole Catholic Church
bishop	the leader of a diocese
priests	ordained ministers who lead and serve us in the Church
deacons	ordained ministers who help with parish work
eucharistic ministers	bring us Holy Communion, especially to the sick
lectors	read to us from the Bible during Mass
altar servers	help the priest at Mass
director of religious education	directs our parish religious education program
Catholic school principal	the leader of our Catholic school
religious sisters	women in religious communities who serve God and others
religious brothers	men in religious communities who serve God and others
pastoral ministers	parish workers who help carry on the mission of Jesus
justice and peace workers	help our parish to work for God's kingdom of justice and peace

Move ahead 2 spaces.
You were kind
to a classmate.

OUR CATHOLIC FAITH

■ We give praise and thanks to God for all those who help our Church community.

■ Tell how the sacraments help us to live as members of Jesus' community.

A Worshiping Community

This year we learned that the sacraments are powerful signs through which Jesus shares God's life and love with us in the community of the Church. By the power of the Holy Spirit, each sacrament helps us to grow in God's life in a special way.

Play this "**Worship Wheel**" game with a partner.

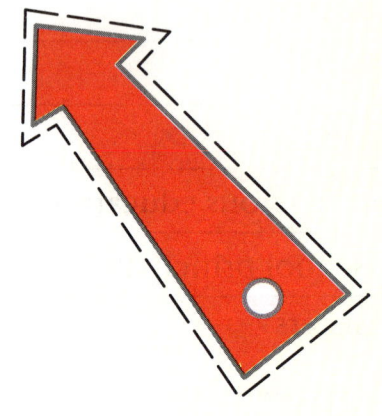

1. Write the name of a sacrament in each wedge of the wheel. The colors of the wedges match the colors of the question cards on page 245, so, write Baptism in the green wedge.

2. Trace the wheel and the spinner on cardboard. Cut out the pieces.

3. Attach the spinner to the wheel.

4. One child spins the spinner and chooses a question about that sacrament. The other child answers.

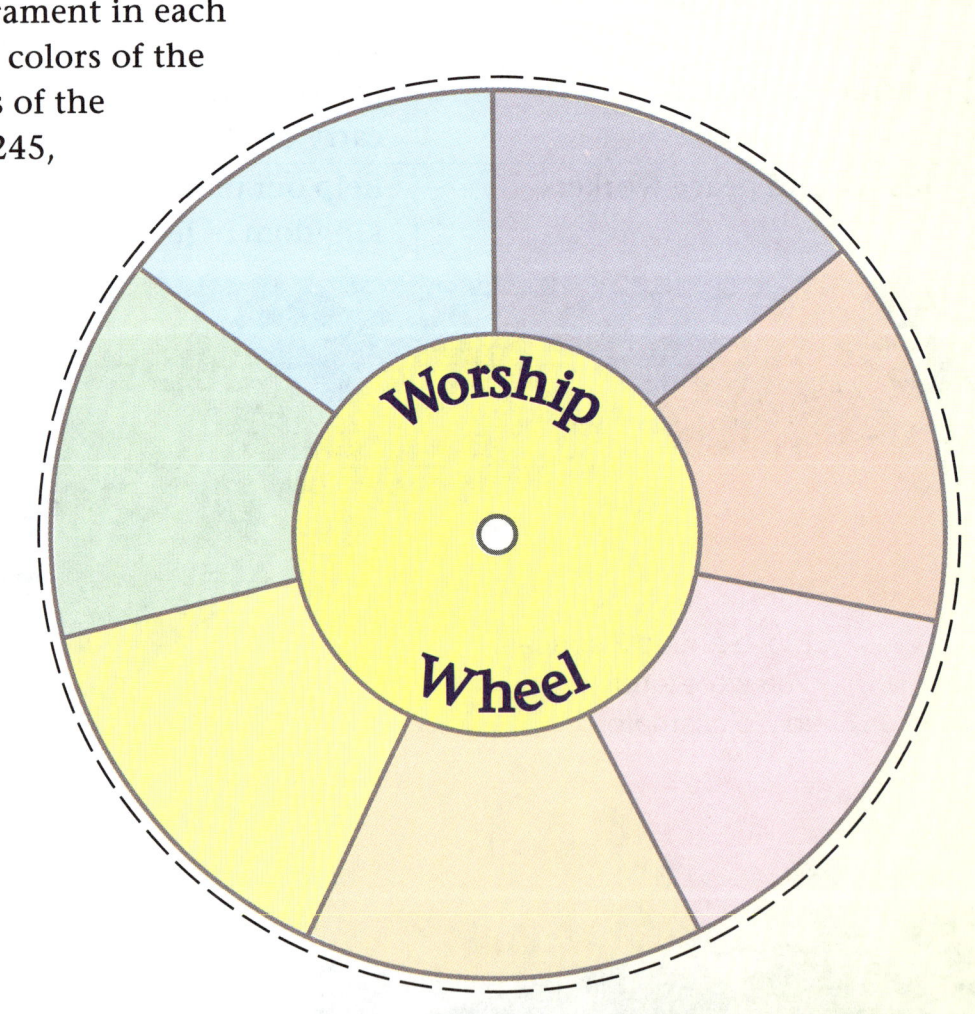

Questions for Worship Wheel Game

Reconciliation

1. Why is Reconciliation called a sacrament of healing?

2. What does Jesus do for us in the sacrament of Reconciliation?

Baptism

1. Why is Baptism called a sacrament of initiation?

2. What does Baptism do for us?

Anointing of the Sick

1. Who should receive the sacrament of the Anointing of the Sick?

2. What does God do for us in the sacrament of the Anointing of the Sick?

Confirmation

1. Who comes to us in a special way in Confirmation?

2. Why is it important to receive Confirmation?

Matrimony

1. How does God bless a man and woman in the sacrament of Matrimony?

2. What does the Church teach us about the family in the sacrament of Matrimony?

Eucharist

1. What does Jesus give us in the Eucharist?

2. Why is the Mass our greatest prayer of praise and thanksgiving?

Holy Orders

1. Why is Holy Orders called a sacrament of service?

2. Why is the sacrament of Holy Orders important?

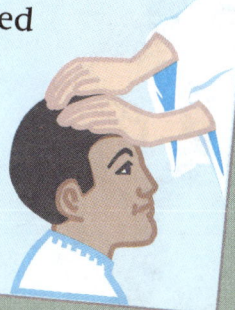

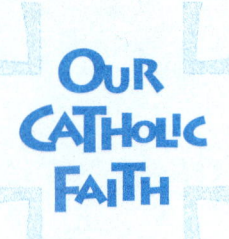

OUR CATHOLIC FAITH

■ Thank You, God, for inviting me to be a member of the Church.

■ Tell some of the ways you know that God is with us always.

God Is with Us Always

This year we learned how important God is in our lives. We learned many things about the Catholic Church. We also learned many ways in which we can show our love for God, others, and ourselves.

It is not always easy to love as we should. We need God's help always.

Here is a coded message. Saying it will help you remember how much God loves and cares for you.

To find the message, look at the guide below. Copy in each space the letter that matches the number.

A	B	C	D	E	F	G
1	2	3	4	5	6	7

H	I	J	K	L	M
8	9	10	11	12	13

N	O	P	Q	R	S
14	15	16	17	18	19

T	U	V	W	X	Y	Z
20	21	22	23	24	25	26

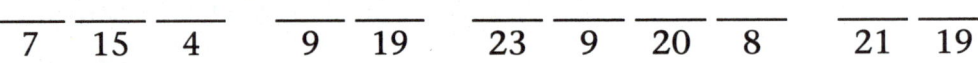

___ ___ ___   ___ ___   ___ ___ ___   ___ ___
7 15   4   9 19   23 9 20 8   21 19

___ ___ ___ ___ ___ ___
1 12 23 1 25 19

The Parish Council

The Catholic Church wants every parish to have a parish council. A parish council is a group of lay people who help the pastor to care for the parish community.

Each council member represents the needs of a particular group in the parish. For example, one council member might serve the needs of elderly parishioners. In some parishes, young people have their own representative on the parish council.

Many wonderful people give their time and talents to be hardworking members of the parish council. Find out who your parish council members are. Say a prayer for them.

Learn by heart **Faith Summary**

- Our Church is a worshiping and caring community.

- We all have a part in building up our Church community and bringing Jesus' good news to others.

COMING TO FAITH

Work together to make "My Catholic Faith Book" on pages 273–276.
Talk over what you have learned this year about:
- what we believe and celebrate.
- the ways we pray and live.
- the ways we serve others.

PRACTICING FAITH

Sing how you will live your faith
during vacation time.

(To the tune of "Clementine")

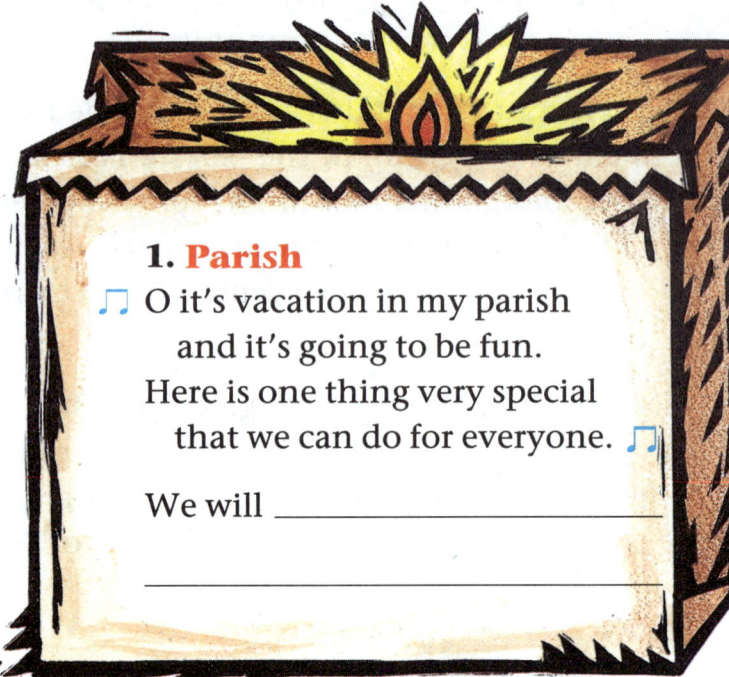

1. Parish
♫ O it's vacation in my parish
  and it's going to be fun.
Here is one thing very special
  that we can do for everyone. ♫

We will _____

_____

2. Family
♫ O my family this vacation
  will be needing my help,
  too.
So when we are all together,
  here is what I plan to do. ♫

I will _____

_____

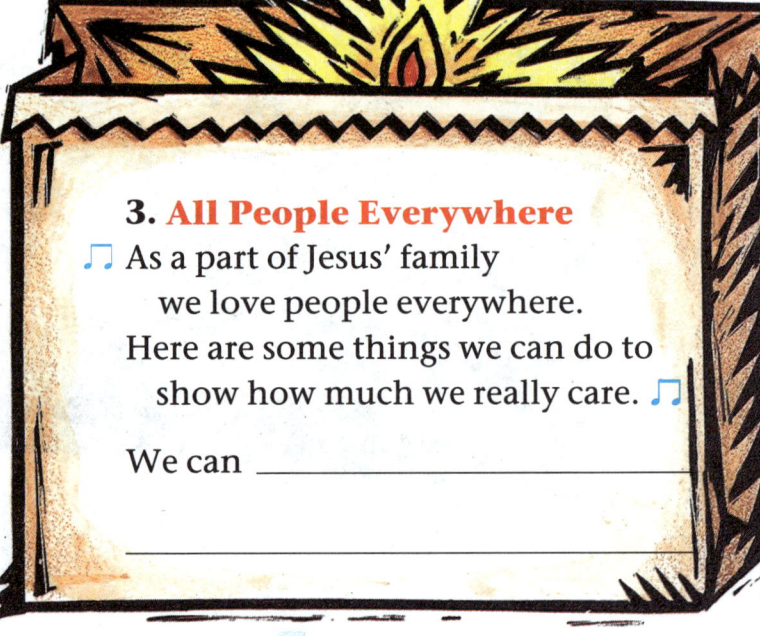

3. All People Everywhere
♫ As a part of Jesus' family
  we love people everywhere.
Here are some things we can do to
  show how much we really care. ♫

We can _____

_____

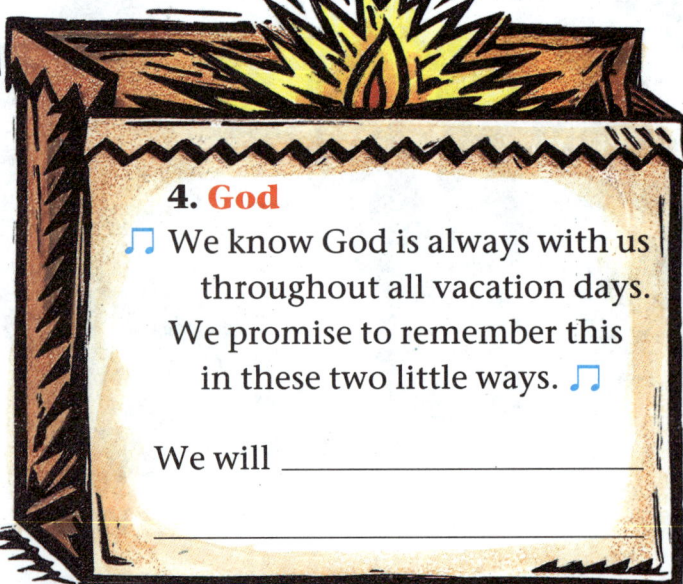

4. God
♫ We know God is always with us
  throughout all vacation days.
We promise to remember this
  in these two little ways. ♫

We will _____

_____

Talk with your teacher
about ways you and
your family might use
the "Faith Alive"
section. Ask your family
to pray the Family
Prayer with you.

REVIEW ▪ TEST

Complete the sentences below.

1. Ordained ministers who help with parish work are

_____ .

2. Persons who read to us from the Bible during Mass are called

_____ .

3. Women in religious communities who serve God and others are

_____ .

4. Persons who bring Holy Communion to sick members of the parish are

_____ .

5. What can you do this week to show one person in your parish that you really care for her or him?

_____

_____

_____

FAITH ALIVE AT HOME AND IN THE PARISH

This lesson helped your child to recall what was learned this year about Jesus, the Church, and the ways we are to live as disciples of Jesus Christ. For your child to grow in faith, it is important that your family take an active part in your parish community and give good example of what it means to belong to the Church.

†Family Prayer

As a family, pray the rosary to thank God for all the blessings you have received this year. Remind your child that while praying each decade of the rosary, we think about a special event (or mystery) in the life of Jesus or Mary. (See pages 236 and 278 for a complete explanation of the rosary.)

Summer Vacation Plans

Go over the activity on page 248. Ask your child to explain her or his plans for living our faith during summer vacation. Share how you, too, will try to grow in love for God, for your family, for your parish, and for all people everywhere. Then sing together how you will live your faith during vacation time. After each verse, have your child read his or her plans and then add your own. If possible, invite the entire family to participate in this activity.

27 Prayer

Lord,
teach us to
pray!

Our Life

The gospels remind us that Jesus often took time to pray. Here is a prayer that Jesus said:

"I thank You, Father, that You listen to Me. I know that You always listen to Me, but I say this for the sake of the people here, so that they will believe that You sent Me."
From John 11:41–42

Do you ever talk to God?

When are your favorite times to pray?

Sharing Life

Imagine you are going to sleep tonight.
What might you say to God?

Imagine you are sick.
What might you say to God?

Imagine you are out in God's beautiful world.
What might you say to God?

Think of another time when you might want to pray to God. What might you say to God?

_____

_____

_____

_____

How does knowing that God always listens to our prayers make you feel? Tell God about it.

In this lesson we will learn more about prayer.

We Will Learn

● We can pray at any time and in any place.

● We can pray with our own words and with the prayers of the Church.

OUR CATHOLIC FAITH

We Talk and Listen to God

We can talk and listen to God in our hearts without saying anything out loud. We can use our own words and talk to God as we would with a best friend.

We can pray kneeling or standing. We can pray sitting or even lying down. We can pray at any time and in any place. In whatever way we pray, we should show reverence to God who is always present with us.

Did you know that we can pray with our bodies as well as with words?

When we enter the church, we genuflect or bow to show reverence for the Blessed Sacrament. During the Mass, the priest sometimes prays with his arms wide open, as if he were praying for the whole world. Sometimes he prays with his hands held up, as if he were waiting for God to fill them. Sometimes he bows low to show reverence in God's presence.

Look at the pictures.
What different ways can we pray, too?

We can also pray with words given to us by the Catholic Church. These are prayers that Catholics have prayed for hundreds and hundreds of years, such as the Our Father and Hail Mary.

Two of the special times we pray to thank God are before and after meals. We think of all the poor and hungry people in the world. We thank God for blessing us with the gift of good food and with many other gifts of love.

What prayers do you know?

COMING TO FAITH

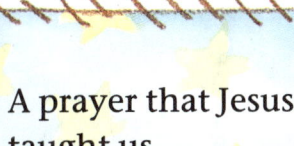

Use these words to fill in the blanks below.

Our Father   Grace Before Meals   Creed

Hail Mary   Act of Contrition   Glory to the Father

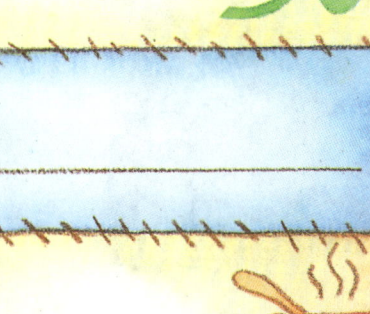

A prayer that Jesus taught us
_____

A prayer we say to Mary
_____

A prayer we say to the Blessed Trinity
_____

A prayer in which we say what we believe
_____

A prayer we say before we eat
_____

A prayer we say to tell God we are sorry
_____

PRACTICING FAITH

Share this blessing with a partner. Take turns praying.

✝ Glory to God our Father, from age to age, in the Church and in Christ Jesus!

Share the sign of peace with your partner after praying the blessing. Change partners until each person in the group has shared the blessing.

Talk with your teacher about ways you and your family might use the "Faith Alive" section. Invite your family to write mini-prayers that you could pray each day.

REVIEW · TEST

Check the circle beside the correct answer.

1. A prayer that Jesus taught us is the
    ○ Apostles' Creed.   ○ Our Father.   ○ Hail Mary.

2. A prayer we say before meals is
    ○ the Our Father.   ○ the Hail Mary.   ○ Grace.

3. We proclaim what we believe in the
    ○ Our Father.   ○ Apostles' Creed.   ○ Act of Contrition.

4. A prayer to tell God we are sorry is the
    ○ Act of Contrition.   ○ Hail Mary.   ○ Sign of the Cross.

5. Do you have a favorite way to pray? Tell about it.

_____

_____

FAITH ALIVE AT HOME AND IN THE PARISH

In this lesson your child learned more about prayer and some of its many forms. Jesus taught His followers many things about prayer. One of His most important teachings was that prayer is the expression of a trusting relationship with God, not the fulfillment of a rule. We find in Jesus a model of someone whose whole life was prayer. Just as Jesus first learned His prayer from Mary and Joseph, so too will your child learn the value and practice of prayer at home.

Mini-Prayers

Encourage your child to develop the habit of being aware of God's presence throughout the day. With your family make up mini-prayers you might say to God at any time each day. Examples: "My Lord and my God;" "Jesus, I know You love me;" "God, You are always with me;" "Holy Spirit, guide me." Together, make up several mini-prayers. Urge each family member to choose one that he or she will try to say every day.

Praying in Silence

Another way to encourage awareness of God's presence in our lives is by praying in silence. Bedtime may be an appropriate time to urge your child to think quietly about her or his day and to recall the signs of God's loving presence. You might guide your child by suggesting that he or she remember the good things that happened today — the rain or sunshine, being with friends at school, learning new things, etc. Help your child to see that God is always with us, loving and caring for us.

Learn by heart **Faith Summary**

- We can pray at any time and in any place.

- We can pray with our own words and with the prayers of the Church.

Lord, make us,
like the saints,
instruments of
Your peace.

Saint Rose of Lima

Patroness of
South America

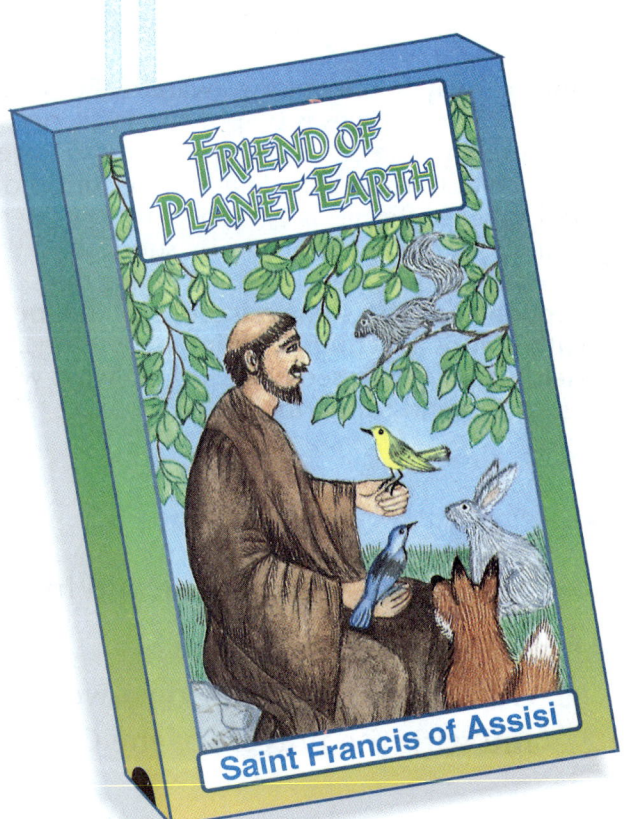

Friend of
Planet Earth

Saint Francis of Assisi

OUR LIFE

Do you have a hero or heroine of faith?
Who are some that you have
learned about?
Write their names here.

_____

_____

_____

_____

Tell what you like best about each one.

SHARING LIFE

What do you think makes someone
a hero or heroine?

How do heroes and heroines help us?

A Busy
Believer

Saint Martha

Join with a partner. Imagine you have been asked to make a TV commercial called *Heroes and Heroines of Faith*.

Choose a saint for your TV commercial. Write his or her name below. Underneath, list reasons why that person is a hero or heroine of faith.

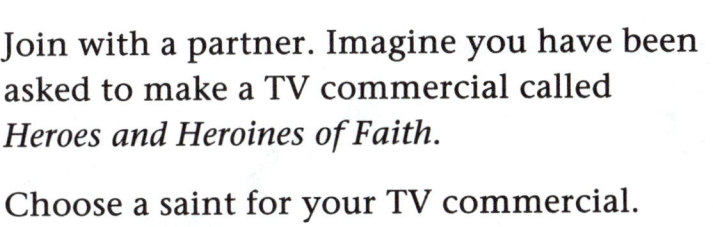

Saint's Name:

_____

Reasons:

_____

_____

_____

_____

On separate paper, write a commercial about your hero or heroine of faith. If you wish, draw pictures to go with the words.

Present your TV commercial to your group. Then display all the commercials under a sign that says "Heroes and Heroines of Faith."

In this lesson we will learn more about the saints.

☀ We Will Learn

- The saints are the heroes and heroines of our Church.

- The lives of the saints show us how to grow as disciples of Jesus.

OUR CATHOLIC FAITH

God's Heroes and Heroines

The saints are the heroes and heroines of our Church. They are examples to us. We do not have to do exactly what they did, but we can be disciples of Jesus with all our hearts as they were. Here are stories about two saints who tried to be all that God asked them to be.

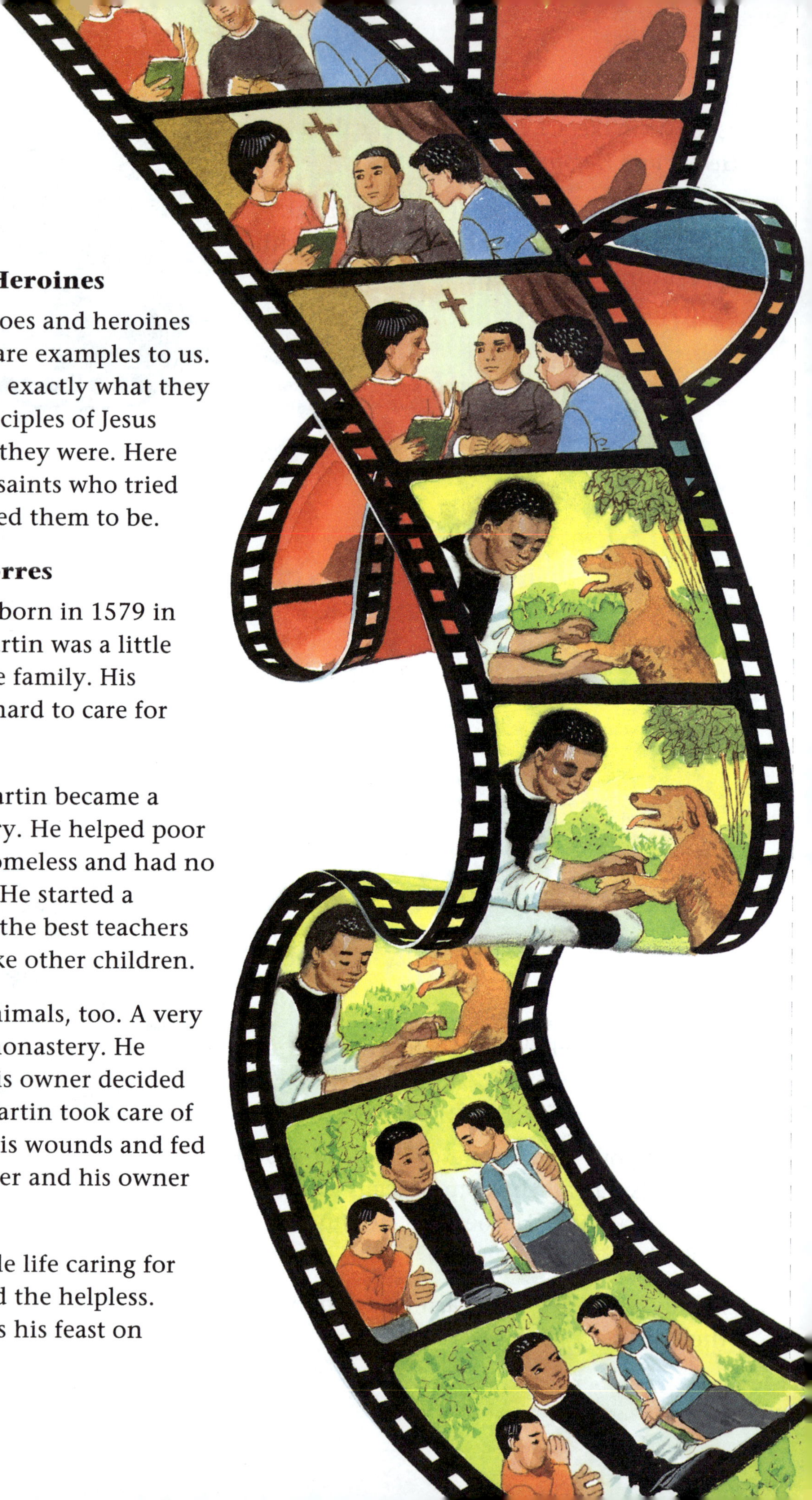

Saint Martin de Porres

Martin de Porres was born in 1579 in Lima, Peru. When Martin was a little boy, his father left the family. His mother worked very hard to care for Martin and his sister.

When he grew up, Martin became a brother in a monastery. He helped poor children who were homeless and had no one to care for them. He started a school for them with the best teachers so they could learn like other children.

Martin was kind to animals, too. A very old dog lived at the monastery. He became so sick that his owner decided to have him killed. Martin took care of the dog. He cleaned his wounds and fed him. The dog got better and his owner decided to keep him.

Martin spent his whole life caring for the poor, the sick, and the helpless. The Church celebrates his feast on November 3.

Martin helps us remember that we are God's children and that Jesus lives in each of us, especially the needy. We try to be kind to others, as Saint Martin was.

Blessed Kateri Tekakwitha

Kateri Tekakwitha was born in 1656. Her father was a fierce Iroquois warrior. When she was a baby, Tekakwitha's parents died suddenly. She was taken in by relatives who were very unkind and treated her like a servant.

Tekakwitha learned about Jesus from some Christians in her tribe. When missionaries came to her camp, she asked to be baptized and took the name Kateri. Many tribe members made fun of Kateri and even threw stones at her.

One dark night, she crept out of camp and traveled by canoe to a Christian village. The Indians there took her in and became her friends. Kateri spent the rest of her short life in prayer and in doing kind things for others.

When you are teased or treated unkindly by others, think of Blessed Kateri. Ask her to ask Jesus to make you strong.

Coming To Faith

Plan a "Celebration of Saints." Perhaps you could dress as your favorite saint and wear a name tag telling who you are.

Each person can tell the group about the chosen saint and why that saint is special. End with a procession of saints and sing a hymn such as "For All the Saints."

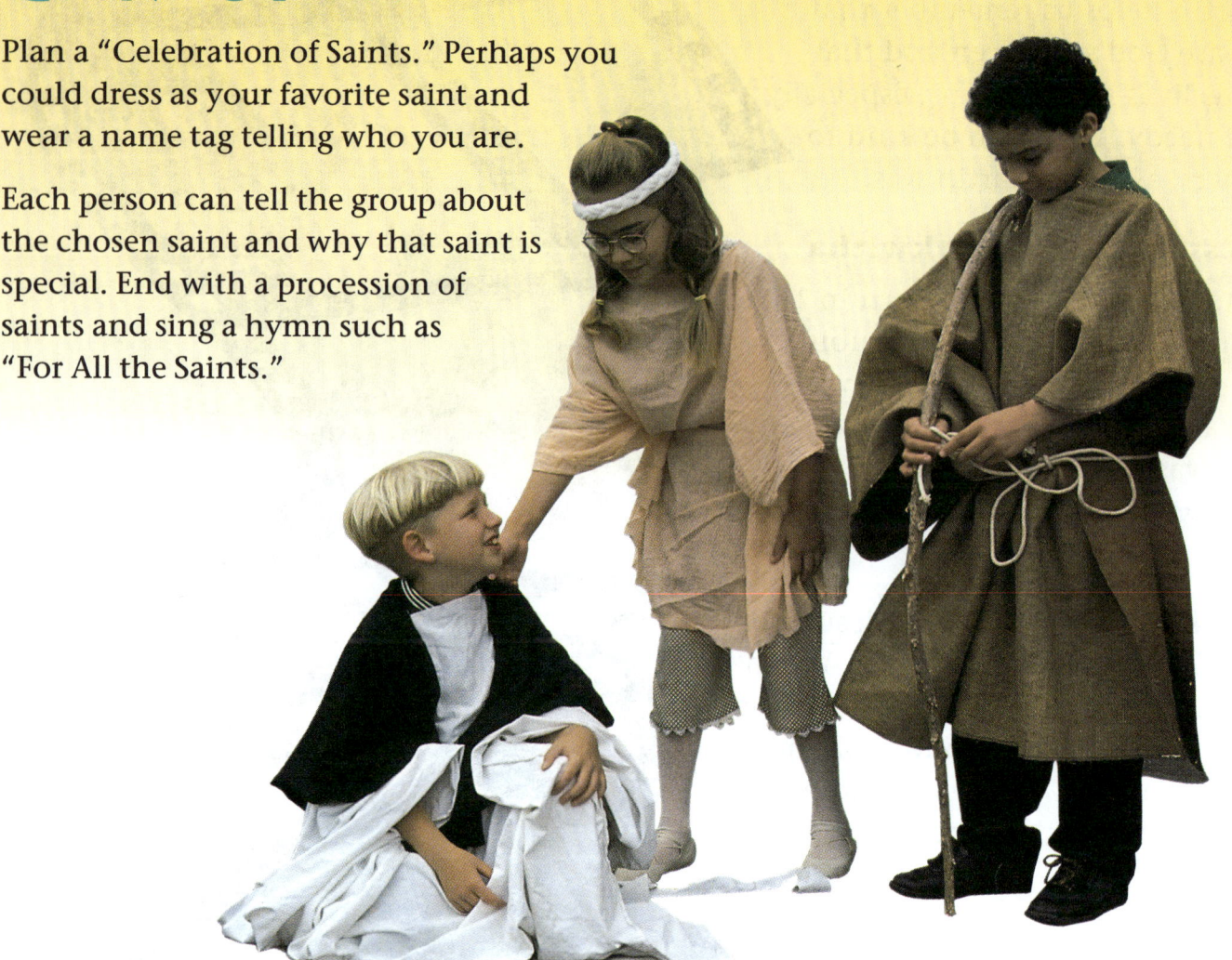

Practicing Faith

Find out all that you can about your patron or your favorite saint.

Write a prayer to your favorite saint. Ask for help to grow more like Jesus. Write one thing you will do to become more like a hero or heroine for God.

_____

_____

_____

Parish, Family, and Me

Jesus is with us always and is our friend. Through Baptism we become disciples of Jesus. We live as Jesus' friends when we care for one another in our family and in our community.

Jesus Calls His Followers

Jesus gathered followers, or disciples, to help carry on His mission. He taught them to love God, others and themselves. Jesus asks us to pray and to be peacemakers. Jesus died on the cross for us. He rose on Easter Sunday to bring us new life.

The Church Begins

Jesus promised to send a Helper. On Pentecost, the Holy Spirit came. God the Holy Spirit gave the disciples courage to share the good news. We first receive the gift of the Holy Spirit at Baptism, then in a special way at Confirmation.

The Church Today

Jesus chose Peter and the other apostles as special leaders in His Church. Today, the pope and bishops continue the work of the apostles. Each of us has a special part to play in the Church to carry on the mission of Jesus.

Our Parish Church

A parish is a group of Jesus' friends who worship God together and care for one another. Our parish is our special home in the Church, the body of Christ. We pray and we worship God in our parish church.

UNIT 1 • TEST

Fill in the missing word or words.

1. Through baptism we become Jesus' _____ .

2. Jesus taught His disciples to love God, _____ ,
and themselves.

3. The Helper sent by Jesus on Pentecost is _____ .

4. Our special home in the Church is called the _____ .

5. What will you do to be a disciple of Jesus?

_____

_____

_____

_____

Child's name_____

Your child has just completed Unit 1. Mark and
return this checklist to the teacher. It will help
both you and the teacher know how to help your
child to grow in faith.

_____ My child needs help with the part of the
Review I have underlined.

_____ My child understands what has been taught
in this unit.

_____ I would like to speak with you. My phone
number is _____ .

(Signature) _____

30 UNIT 2 · REVIEW

Our Parish Prays

Prayer is talking and listening to God. We pray to Mary and to the other saints. We pray for all the living and the dead. We are all united in our Church by Baptism.

Our Parish Worships

We worship God through the seven sacraments. The sacraments of initiation welcome us into the Church community. The sacraments of healing and service help us to love and serve one another.

Our Parish Celebrates Forgiveness

Sometimes we do not love God and others as Jesus wants us to love them. We sin by freely choosing to do what we know is wrong; we disobey God's law on purpose. God forgives us in the sacrament of Reconciliation. Jesus wants us to forgive others as we have been forgiven.

Our Parish Prepares for Mass

The Mass is our greatest prayer of praise and thanks to God. At Mass, Jesus gives us the gift of Himself to be our food. We each have a part to play in the Mass.

Our Parish Celebrates the Mass

Our parish family gathers for the celebration of the Mass. In the Liturgy of the Word, we listen to God. In the Liturgy of the Eucharist, our gifts of bread and wine become the Body and Blood of Christ. At the end of Mass we go in peace to love and serve others.

UNIT 2 ▪ TEST

Fill in the missing word or words.

1. We are made members of the Church in the sacrament
of _____.

2. When we freely choose to disobey God's Law, we _____.

3. In the Liturgy of the _____, we listen to
readings from the Bible.

4. The _____ are powerful signs through which Jesus
shares God's life and love with us.

5. How can you take part in the Mass more fully?

_____

_____

_____

_____

Child's name_____

Your child has just completed Unit 2. Mark and
return this checklist to the teacher. It will help
both you and the teacher know how to help your
child to grow in faith.

_____ My child needs help with the part of the
Review I have underlined.

_____ My child understands what has been taught
in this unit.

_____ I would like to speak with you. My phone
number is _____.

(Signature) _____

Jesus Christ Gives Us His Church

Jesus wants us to live together as a loving community. He taught His disciples to love God, one another, and themselves. Jesus gave His life for us. On Easter Sunday, He rose from the dead to bring us new life.

On Pentecost, Jesus sent God the Holy Spirit to His disciples to help them spread the good news. The Holy Spirit helps us live as disciples of Jesus.

We each have an important part to play in bringing about the kingdom, or reign, of God. Jesus chose leaders for His Church. The pope and bishops continue their leadership today.

We Live the Way of Jesus in Our Parish

Prayer is talking and listening to God. We also ask Mary and the other saints to pray for us. We pray for the living and the dead.

We worship God through the sacraments. The sacraments are powerful signs through which Jesus shares God's life and love with us.

Sometimes we sin. We do not love God and others as we should. When we are truly sorry, God always forgives us. We celebrate God's love and forgiveness in the sacrament of Reconciliation.

The Mass is our greatest prayer of praise and thanks to God. At Mass we remember and celebrate Jesus' life, death, and resurrection. The two main parts of the Mass are the *Liturgy of the Word* and the *Liturgy of the Eucharist*.

FIRST SEMESTER ▪ TEST

Circle the letter beside the correct answer.

1. Jesus taught His disciples to
   a. work miracles.
   b. love one another.
   c. be important.

2. Jesus rose from the dead on
   a. Christmas Day.
   b. Pentecost Sunday.
   c. Easter Sunday.

3. A sacrament that brings us God's forgiveness is
   a. Reconciliation.
   b. Confirmation.
   c. Holy Orders.

4. Jesus sent the Holy Spirit to His disciples on
   a. Pentecost.
   b. Easter.
   c. Christmas.

5. The Helper Jesus sent to the Church is the
   a. pope.
   b. bishop.
   c. Holy Spirit.

Think and respond:
Tell some ways you can pray, both alone and with others.

_____

_____

_____

Our Church and the Bible

The Bible is the story of God's love for us. In the Old Testament we read about what God did for Abraham and Sarah's descendants. The New Testament tells us about the life, death, and resurrection of Jesus and His mission.

Our Church Shares the Good News

The first Christians told the good news of God's love to everyone. Today, missionaries carry the good news of Jesus Christ all over the world. We can be missionaries in our home, our parish, and our neighborhood.

Our Church as a Community

The pope is the leader of the whole Catholic Church. Each diocese is led by a bishop, and each parish is led by a pastor. A vocation is an invitation to serve God and the Church in a special way.

Our Church Works for Justice and Peace

Jesus welcomed everyone into His community of disciples. Today the Catholic Church welcomes everyone and defends the rights of those who are treated unfairly.

Our Church and the Kingdom

God's kingdom, or reign, is the power of God's life and love in the world. We are all called to be signs of God's kingdom by doing God's will.

UNIT 3 ▪ TEST

Complete each of the sentences below.

1. A group of Catholic parishes led by a bishop is called

a _____.

2. People who bring the good news to others in countries all over the

world are called _____.

3. The leader of the whole Church is the _____.

4. An invitation to serve God and the Church in a special way

is called a _____.

5. What can you do to build up God's kingdom in your parish?

_____

_____

_____

Child's name_____

Your child has just completed Unit 3. Mark and return this checklist to the teacher. It will help both you and the teacher know how to help your child to grow in faith.

_____ My child needs help with the part of the Review I have underlined.

_____ My child understands what has been taught in this unit.

_____ I would like to speak with you. My phone number is _____.

(Signature) _____

33 UNIT 4 · REVIEW

The Church Is One and Holy

The Church is one, holy, catholic, and apostolic. To be one means that we are united in one faith and love. Our Church is holy. We put God first when we live as Jesus taught us.

The Church Is Catholic and Apostolic

Our Church is catholic. Catholic means that all people are invited to belong to it. Our Church is apostolic. Our Pope and bishops carry on the mission Jesus gave to the apostles. As followers of Jesus, we help the Church show its four signs, or marks, to others.

We Are All God's People

God wants us to love and respect all people. Through the Jewish people, we received our belief in the one true God. All Christians are our sisters and brothers in Christ. We work for unity among all Christians.

Mary, Mother of the Church

Mary, Mother of God, is our mother, too. She is the Mother of all Christians. We celebrate many feast days to honor Mary.

We Are the Church

Our Church is the people of God. We all have a part to play in building up the Church. The sacraments help us to grow in God's life. God is always with us.

UNIT 4 ▪ TEST

Circle the letter next to the correct answer.

1. The Church is one means that our Church
   a. is united in faith and love.
   b. respects people of all faiths.
   c. is holy.

2. The Church is apostolic means that
   a. we put God first.
   b. we carry out Jesus' mission.
   c. the Church has four signs or marks.

3. We should respect all people because
   a. we all worship God in the same way.
   b. we are all Christians.
   c. God created all people.

4. The immaculate conception of Mary means that
   a. Mary said yes to God.
   b. Mary was born free of original sin.
   c. Mary visited her cousin Elizabeth.

5. How will you live as a follower of Jesus?

   _____

   _____

   _____

   _____

34 SECOND SEMESTER · REVIEW

Our Church and Our Parish

The Bible is the story of God's people. We find stories about the people of Israel in the Old Testament. The New Testament tells us about Jesus Christ and His mission.

The Church spreads the good news of Jesus everywhere. In the Catholic Church the pope, bishops, and pastors lead and serve us in special ways. We are all called to serve others and work together.

Jesus invites everyone to belong to His community. Our Church teaches us to be just and fair and to be peacemakers. When we do God's will, we are signs of the kingdom, or reign, of God.

United in Our Catholic Church

The Church is one. We are and try to be united in one faith and in love for one another. The Church is holy. We are holy when we try to put God first in our lives. The Church is catholic. We try to welcome all people and bring the good news everywhere. The Church is apostolic. The Church shows that it is apostolic by being faithful to the mission Jesus gave to the apostles.

Through the Jewish people we received our belief in the one true God. All Christians are our brothers and sisters in Jesus Christ. We work for unity among all Christians.

We honor Mary, the Mother of God. We call her the Mother of the Church and our mother, too.

SECOND SEMESTER ▪ TEST

Fill in the missing word or words.

1. The _____ is made up of the Old Testament and the New Testament.

2. A _____ is an invitation to serve God and the Church in a special way.

3. Our Church works for _____ and justice.

4. The _____ ____ _____ is the power of God's life and love in the world.

5. The Church is _____ means that we are united in faith and love.

6. The Church is _____ means that we try to live holy lives.

7. The Church is _____ means that the Church is all over the world with a message important for all.

8. The Church is _____ means that it shows it is faithful to the mission Jesus gave to the apostles.

9. The Blessed Virgin Mary is the mother of _____ , and our mother, too.

10. Tell how you will show that you are a disciple of Jesus and a member of the Church.

My Catholic Faith Book

For the Family

As your child's third grade experience ends, we celebrate with you the ways in which your child has been a sign of the kingdom, or reign, of God. You have guided your child's growth in the wisdom of Christian faith, including a love for Scripture. During this year, your child has learned and experienced some very important truths of our faith as they are contained in the *Catechism of the Catholic Church*. For example:

• **Creed:** We believe in the Blessed Trinity. God the Holy Spirit, the third Person of the Blessed Trinity, continues to help the Church today. We believe that the Church is one, holy, catholic, and apostolic. The Holy Spirit strengthens us and gives us courage to say and do the right thing as disciples of Jesus Christ.

• **Sacraments:** By the power of the Holy Spirit, the Church celebrates seven sacraments. The sacraments of initiation are Baptism, Confirmation, and Eucharist. The sacraments of healing are Anointing of the Sick and Reconciliation. The sacraments of service are Holy Orders and Matrimony.

• **Morality:** We are disciples of Jesus by following His teaching in the Law of Love—to love God, others, and ourselves.

• **Prayer:** We pray when we praise God, thank God, ask God for help, or ask God's forgiveness when we are sorry for our sins. We pray by ourselves or with our parish community in our own words or in words taught to us by Jesus and the Church.

Continue to encourage your child to be a sign of the kingdom, or reign, of God by going to Mass together, singing the faith songs, reading Bible stories, and praying together.

† Family Prayer

Dear God,
Help our family to continue to grow in faith each day. God, help us as we try to say and do the right thing as disciples of Jesus Christ, Your Son. Amen.

This is what we believe . . .

Jesus is always with us. Through Baptism we become disciples of Jesus.

Jesus gathered followers, or disciples, to help carry on His mission. Jesus chose Peter and the other apostles as special leaders in His Church. Today, the pope and bishops continue the work of the apostles.

Jesus died on the cross out of love for us. He rose on Easter Sunday to bring us new life.

Jesus promised to send a Helper. The Holy Spirit came to the disciples on Pentecost.

God the Holy Spirit continues to help the Church today. The Holy Spirit strengthens us to live our faith. The Holy Spirit gives us courage to say and to do the right thing as disciples of Jesus.

Jesus invites everyone to belong to His community. The Church spreads the good news of Jesus everywhere. We are all called to do God's loving will—to be signs of the kingdom, or reign, of God.

This is how we pray . . .

We pray when we praise God, thank God, ask God for help, or ask God's forgiveness when we are sorry for our sins. We pray by ourselves or with our parish community.

We pray in our own words or we pray the prayers of the Church, such as the Glory to the Father. We pray using the words Jesus taught us when we say the Our Father. When we tell God we are sorry for our sins, we pray an Act of Contrition. We say what we believe as Christians when we pray the Creed.

We pray to Mary, the Mother of God, when we pray the Hail Mary, the greeting of the angel to Mary. We remember the events from the lives of Jesus and Mary when we pray the rosary.

We ask Mary and the other saints to pray for us. We remember to pray for the living and the dead.

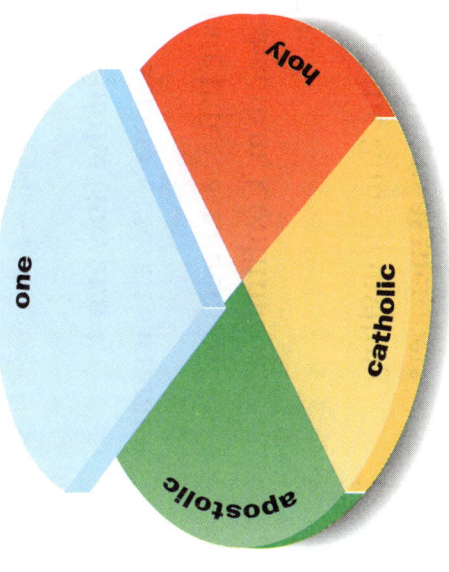

one
holy
catholic
apostolic

The Church is one in Jesus. We are one because we are united in faith and in love for one another.

The Church is holy in Jesus. We are holy because we share in God's life.

The Church is catholic in Jesus. We are catholic because we welcome all people and bring the good news everywhere.

The Church is apostolic in Jesus. We are apostolic because we remain faithful to the mission Jesus gave to the apostles.

Mary is the Mother of God. We call her the Mother of the Church and our mother, too.

This is how we live . . .

M The Holy Spirit guides and helps us in trying to live as Jesus' friends. We are disciples of Jesus by following His teaching in the Law of Love—to love God, others, and ourselves.

O We care for one another in our family and our community. We pray and worship together at Mass. At the end of Mass, we are sent to love and serve the Lord and one another.

R

A

L We try not to sin, to disobey God's law on purpose. We forgive those who have hurt us, and we ask forgiveness of those we have hurt.

I

T We each have an important part to play in bringing about the kingdom, or reign of God. We try to live as peacemakers, as Jesus taught us.

Y

4

This is how we celebrate . . .

By the power of the Holy Spirit, the Church celebrates seven sacraments.

S We celebrate three sacraments of initiation: Baptism, Confirmation, and Eucharist.

A We celebrate the Church inviting us and welcoming us as members.

C In Baptism we are freed from sin, become children of God, and are welcomed as members of the Church.

R In Confirmation the Holy Spirit comes to us in a special way to give us courage to live as Jesus' disciples.

A In the Eucharist the bread and wine become the Body and Blood of Christ at Mass. Jesus is really present in the Eucharist. We receive Jesus Himself in Holy Communion.

M We celebrate two sacraments of healing: Reconciliation and Anointing of the Sick.

E In Reconciliation we celebrate God's love and forgiveness of our sins.

N In Anointing of the Sick the Church brings God's own healing and peace to the sick.

T We celebrate two sacraments of service: Holy Orders and Matrimony.

S In Holy Orders the Church chooses men to be ordained ministers and to serve as bishops, priests, and deacons.

In Matrimony God blesses the love and marriage of a man and a woman. Through their love, they serve each other, the Church, and the world.

The Mass is our greatest prayer of praise and thanks to God. It is both a meal and a sacrifice. At Mass we remember and celebrate Jesus' life, death, and resurrection. The two main parts of the Mass are the *Liturgy of the Word* and the *Liturgy of the Eucharist*.

PRAYERS AND PRACTICES

Our Father

Our Father, who art in heaven,
hallowed be thy name;
thy kingdom come;
thy will be done on earth
as it is in heaven.
Give us this day our daily bread;
and forgive us our trespasses
as we forgive those
who trespass against us;
and lead us not into temptation,
but deliver us from evil. Amen.

Hail Mary

Hail Mary, full of grace,
the Lord is with you;
blessed are you among women,
and blessed is the fruit
of your womb, Jesus.
Holy Mary, Mother of God,
pray for us sinners now
and at the hour of our death. Amen.

Act of Contrition

My God,
I am sorry for my sins with all my heart.
In choosing to do wrong
and failing to do good,
I have sinned against you,
whom I should love above all things.
I firmly intend, with your help,
to do penance, to sin no more,
and to avoid whatever leads me to sin.
Our Savior Jesus Christ
suffered and died for us.
In his name, my God, have mercy.

Apostles' Creed

I believe in God,
the Father Almighty,
creator of heaven and earth.

I believe in Jesus Christ,
his only Son, our Lord.
He was conceived
by the power
of the Holy Spirit
and born of the Virgin Mary.
He suffered under Pontius
Pilate, was crucified,
died, and was buried.
He descended to the dead.
On the third day he rose again.
He ascended into heaven,
and is seated at the right hand
of the Father.
He will come again to judge
the living and the dead.

I believe in the Holy Spirit,
the holy catholic Church,
the communion of saints,
the forgiveness of sins,
the resurrection of the body,
and the life everlasting.
Amen.

Glory to the Father

Glory to the Father, and to the Son,
and to the Holy Spirit:
as it was in the beginning,
is now, and will be for ever. Amen.

Hail, Holy Queen

Hail, Holy Queen, Mother of Mercy;
hail, our life, our sweetness,
and our hope! To you do we cry,
poor banished children of Eve;
to you do we send up our sighs,
mourning and weeping in this vale of tears.
Turn, then, most gracious advocate,
your eyes of mercy toward us;
and after this our exile, show unto us
the blessed fruit of your womb, Jesus,
O clement, O loving, O sweet Virgin Mary!

Morning Offering

O loving God, I give you this day
All that I think and do and say,
Uniting it with what was done
On earth, by Jesus Christ, your Son.

Grace Before Meals

Bless us, O Lord,
and these your gifts,
which we are about to receive
from your bounty,
through Christ our Lord. Amen.

Grace After Meals

We give you thanks, almighty God,
for these and all your gifts
which we have received through
Christ our Lord. Amen.

Prayer for My Vocation

Dear God,
You have a great and loving plan
for our world and for me.
I wish to share in that plan fully,
faithfully, and joyfully.

Help me to understand what it is
you wish me to do with my life.
Help me to be attentive to the signs
that you give me about preparing
for the future.

And once I have heard and understood
your call, give me the strength
and the grace to follow it
with generosity and love. Amen.

The Rosary

A rosary has a cross, followed by one large bead and three small ones. Then there is a circle with five "decades." Each decade consists of one large bead followed by ten smaller beads. Begin the rosary with the sign of the cross. Recite the Apostles' Creed. Then pray one Our Father, three Hail Marys, and one Glory to the Father.

To recite each decade, say one Our Father on the large bead and ten Hail Marys on the ten smaller beads. After each decade, pray the Glory to the Father. As you pray each decade, think of the appropriate Joyful, Sorrowful, or Glorious Mystery, a special event in the life of Jesus or Mary. The rosary concludes with the Hail, Holy Queen prayer.

The Five Joyful Mysteries

1. The annunciation
2. The visitation
3. The birth of Jesus
4. The presentation of Jesus in the Temple
5. The finding of Jesus in the Temple

The Five Sorrowful Mysteries

1. The agony in the garden
2. The scourging at the pillar
3. The crowning with thorns
4. The carrying of the cross
5. The crucifixion and death of Jesus

The Five Glorious Mysteries

1. The resurrection
2. The ascension
3. The Holy Spirit comes upon the apostles
4. The assumption of Mary into heaven
5. The coronation of Mary in heaven

Catholics have a custom of praying the mysteries of the rosary as follows: the joyful mysteries on Mondays, Thursdays, and the Sundays of Advent; the sorrowful mysteries on Tuesdays, Fridays, and the Sundays of Lent; and the glorious mysteries on Wednesdays, Saturdays, and the remaining Sundays of the year.

The Stations of the Cross

1. Jesus is condemned to die.
2. Jesus takes up His cross.
3. Jesus falls the first time.
4. Jesus meets His Mother.
5. Simon helps Jesus carry His cross.
6. Veronica wipes the face of Jesus.
7. Jesus falls the second time.
8. Jesus meets the women of Jerusalem.
9. Jesus falls the third time.
10. Jesus is stripped of His garments.
11. Jesus is nailed to the cross.
12. Jesus dies on the cross.
13. Jesus is taken down from the cross.
14. Jesus is laid in the tomb.

Holy Water

A holy water font containing blessed water is placed near the door of the church. When we enter the church, we put our fingers into the holy water and then make the sign of the cross. The water reminds us of our Baptism, and the prayer we say expresses our belief in the Blessed Trinity. Many Catholic families also have holy water in their homes.

Holy Places

We treat places of prayer (churches, synagogues, temples, and mosques) with reverence. In our Catholic churches, we genuflect toward the tabernacle as we enter our pew. Genuflecting (touching our right knee to the floor) is a sign of our reverence for Jesus Christ, who is really present in the Blessed Sacrament.

Visits to the Blessed Sacrament

Before Mass on Sundays or at other special times, take a few minutes to visit Jesus, present in the Blessed Sacrament. After you have taken your place in church, kneel or sit quietly. Be very still. Talk to Jesus about your needs and your hopes. Thank Jesus for His great love. Remember to pray for your family and your parish, especially anyone who is sick or in need.

Closing Prayer Service

Call to Prayer (All): In the name of the Father, and of the Son, and of the Holy Spirit. Amen.

Teacher: As we bring our third grade year to a close, we remember that we have learned many things about Jesus, about Jesus' community, the Church, and about ourselves. Let us listen carefully to some of the things Jesus has taught us.

Jesus: I call you friends. As I have loved you, so you must love one another. Everyone will know that you are my friends if you love one another.
From John 15:15 and John 13:34–35

Narrator: We thank You, Jesus, for making us Your friends and Your disciples in the Church.

All: Help us to love one another, especially all in need.

Jesus: Where two or three come together in My name, I am there with them.
Matthew 18:20

Narrator: We thank You, Jesus, for our parish, where we come together in Your name.

All: Help us to love and serve You and each other always.

Saint Paul: There is one Lord, one faith, one Baptism. There is one God of all who works through all of us.
From Ephesians 4:5–6

Narrator: We thank You, Jesus, for the Church— one, holy, catholic, and apostolic.

All: Help us to live our faith and our baptism, so that God can work through us.

Teacher: Do you remember when Jesus sent His disciples to the whole world? Now Jesus is sending us, His disciples today, to share the good news of God's love with our world. Let us journey together, holding our religion books, and celebrate by singing a song of discipleship.

Teacher: Do you remember when we planted our seeds early in the year? We watered them to help them grow. Today we will use holy water as a sign of our baptism. All during our lives, we grow in God's grace and God's love. Let us each touch this life-giving water and make the sign of the cross. Let us ask God to help us grow in faith and love. Let us ask God to help us bring love and peace to the world.

Now let us renew our willingness to live as disciples of Jesus in the Church by repeating after me:

I will help build God's kingdom. Each day, no matter how hard it is,

I will try to bring God's love and peace to at least one other person.

Let us begin by sharing a sign of peace with one another.

As we end our celebration, let us say the prayer Jesus taught all His disciples: "Our Father. . . ."

Advent (page 128)

The name we give to the four weeks of waiting time before celebrating Jesus' birth at Christmas. We continue to wait until Jesus comes again.

Amen (page 121)

Prayer word meaning "Yes, I believe."

Apostolic (page 214)

Means that the Church is founded on the apostles and is faithful to the mission and beliefs Jesus gave them.

Baptism (page 90)

The sacrament by which we are freed from sin, become children of God, and are welcomed as members of the Church.

Bible (page 140)

The book in which we read the word of God for our lives.

Bishop (page 160)

A bishop is the leader of a diocese.

Blessed Sacrament (page 59)

Another name for the Eucharist. Jesus is really present in the Blessed Sacrament.

Blessed Trinity (page 205)

The three Persons in one God: God the Father, God the Son, and God the Holy Spirit.

Canonized (page 81)

Being named a saint by the Church.

Catholic (page 213)

Means that the Church welcomes all people and has a message for all people.

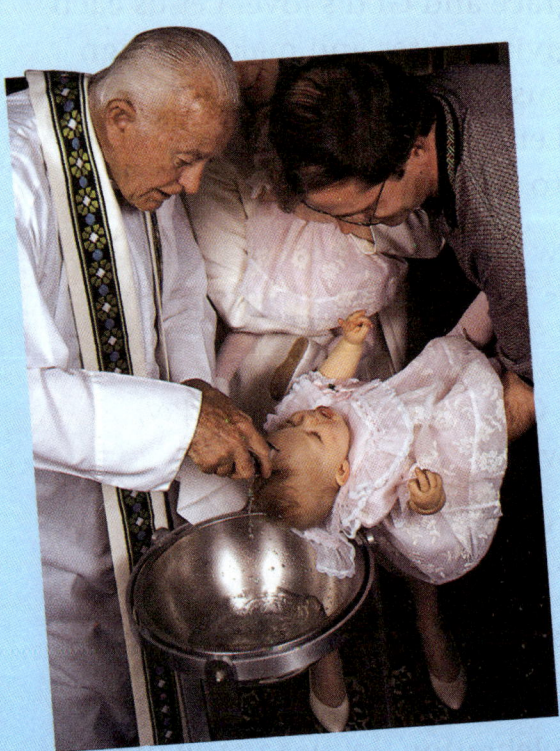

Christians (page 204)

All those who are baptized and believe in and follow Jesus Christ.

Church (pages 20, 204)

The community of Jesus' disciples; the body of Christ.

Communion of Saints (page 82)

The union of all the friends of Jesus, living and dead.

Confession (page 101)

Telling our sins to the priest in the sacrament of Reconciliation.

Creed (page 204)

A summary of our Catholic faith from the early Church.

Disciples (page 10)

The followers of Jesus.

Gospel (page 143)

The good news that God loves us and gives us Jesus Christ, the Son of God.

Grace (page 88)

God's life and love in us.

Holy Spirit (page 37)

God, the third Person of the Blessed Trinity.

Immaculate Conception (page 233)

Mary's privilege of being free from original sin from the first moment of her life.

Initiation (page 90)

Being welcomed into the Church, the community of faith.

Justice (page 171)

A virtue that calls us to treat everyone fairly.

Kingdom, or Reign of God (page 181)

The power of God's life and love in the world.

Law of Love (page 28)

The Law of Love is, "You must love God with all your heart. You must love others as you love yourself."

Lent (page 190)

The special time before Easter. We pray for those preparing for Baptism and try to grow in God's grace as disciples of Jesus Christ.

Liturgy of the Eucharist (page 120)

The part of the Mass in which our gifts of bread and wine are offered to God and become the Body and Blood of Christ.

Liturgy of the Word (page 119)

The part of the Mass in which we listen to readings from the Bible.

Marks of the Church (page 203)
The four marks of the Church are: one, holy, catholic, and apostolic.

Mass (page 109)
Our celebration of Jesus' special meal and sacrifice.

Minister (page 50)
Means "one who serves."

Mission (page 27)
Jesus' mission was His work of bringing the good news of God's love to the world. Our mission is the work we are sent to do in Jesus' name.

Missionary (page 151)
Someone who carries the good news of Jesus Christ to others.

Parish (page 17)
A group of Jesus' disciples who worship God together.

Pentecost (page 39)
The day on which the Church celebrates the coming of the Holy Spirit to the disciples.

Pope (page 49)
The successor of Saint Peter and the leader of the whole Catholic Church.

Rite (page 225)
A part of the Catholic Church that has its own liturgy, laws, and customs.

Sacraments (page 89)
Powerful signs through which Jesus Christ shares God's life and love with us in the community of the Church.

Saints (page 80)
Followers of Jesus Christ who loved God very much, who did God's will on earth and who are now happy with God forever in heaven.

Sin (page 98)
The act of freely choosing to do what we know to be wrong; we disobey God's law on purpose.

Vocation (page 163)
An invitation to serve God and the Church in a special way.

INDEX

Bold-faced pages indicate chapters   *Italics* refer to definitions   285

Italics refer to definitions

Acknowledgments

Grateful acknowledgment is due the following for their work on the New Catholic School Edition of *Coming to the Church*:

Joan B. Collins, Assistant Editor-in-Chief
Joanna Dailey and Beverly Malone, Editors
Tresse De Lorenzo, Manager: Production/Art
Joe Svadlenka, Art Director
Stuart Vance, Manager: Electronic Art/Production
Barbara Brown, Project Manager
Matt Straub, Designer
Jim Saylor, Photo Editor
Mary Kate Coudal, Photo Research

Excerpts and adaptations from *Good News Bible*, copyright © American Bible Society 1966, 1971, 1976, 1979.

Excerpts from the English translation of *The Roman Missal* © 1973, International Committee on English in the Liturgy, Inc. (ICEL); excerpts from the English translation of *Rite of Penance* © 1974, ICEL; excerpts from the English translation of *Rite of Confirmation* © 1975, ICEL. All rights reserved.

Cover Photos

Myrleen Cate: *insets.*
The Wildlife Collection/Charles Gurche: *background and nature insets.*

Photo Credits

Diane J. Ali: 172/173 *background.*
Dennis Barnes: 100 *bottom.*
Myrleen Cate: 18, 19, 20 *top,* 34, 35, 46, 47, 48, 56, 57, 60, 61 *bottom,* 66, 67, 70 *center,* 70 *bottom,* 72, 73, 74, 77 *bottom,* 78 *top* inset, 78/79, 79 *background,* 79 *top,* 79 *bottom,* 81 *bottom,* 86, 87, 98, 99, 100 *top,* 101, 102, 107 *top,* 107 *left,* 108 *bottom,* 118 *bottom,* 120, 121 *top,* 122, 123 *bottom,* 124, 127, 128, 130, 139 *background,* 144, 146, 154 *top,* 162 *top,* 174 *top,* 186, 191, 192, 196, 206, 208, 218, 226 *top,* 238, 250, 252, 254, 260.
Catholic News Service: 165 *bottom,* 214 *top;* Arturo Mari: 50; Joe Rimkus, Jr.: 160 *top.*
Catholic Relief Services: 49 *top,* 212 *top;* Sean Sprague 173 *top.*
CROSIERS/Gene Plaisted, OSC: 40, 49 *bottom,* 56/57, 61 *top,* 61 *right,* 81 *top,* 90, 91 *top,* 92, 107 *right,* 108/109, 110, 118 *top,* 119, 123 *top,* 160 *bottom,* 173 *bottom,* 190 *top,* 210 *top right,* 215, 216, 230, 247.
Leo de Wys, Inc.: Sipa/Sams, 155 *left;* Alan Reininger: 221 *top;* Steve Vidler: 237.
Kathy Ferguson: 145.
FPG International/E.Nagele: 78/79 *background;* Richard Johnston: 148/149 *background;* Spencer Grant: 172 *bottom;* Farrell Grehan: 185 *top;* E. Manewal: 220 *right;* Galen Rowell: 221 *bottom.*
Franciscan Friars of the Atonement - Graymoor: 226 *bottom.*
The Granger Collection: 213.
Ken Karp: 71, 164.
LIAISON International/Wendy Stone: 151 *top;* Gamma Press Images: 151 *bottom,* 212 *bottom;* Livio Anticoli: 222 *bottom.*
Eric Lessing/Magnum: 165 *top.*
Maryknoll/F.D. Hessler: 152/153; Fr. Fern Gosselin: 155 *right.*
Lawrence Migdale: 70 *top.*
Our Lady of the Mississippi Abbey, Dubuque, IA: 185 *bottom.*
Our Lady of the Most Holy Rosary Catholic Community, Albuquerque, NM: 54.
Sarma Ozols: 257.
Frances Roberts: 214 *bottom.*
H. Armstrong Roberts: 78 *background,* 210 *bottom left,* 228 *bottom.*
James L. Shaffer: 91 *bottom,* 108 *top,* 121 *bottom.*
Nancy Sheehan: 190 *bottom.*
Chris Sheridan: 21, 109, 154 *bottom.*
Stock Boston/Bob Daemmrich: 174 *bottom.*
The Stock Market/Paul Barton: 20 *bottom;* Gabe Palmer: 77 *top.*
The Stock Solution/Robert C. Dawson: 228 *top.*
Matt Straub: 153.
Tony Stone Images: 211; Jeff Zaruba: 152; David Joel: 162 *bottom;* Marcus Brooke 210 *top left;*: Ric Ergenbright: 217; Don Smetzer: 220 *left;* Bushnell/Soifer: 221 *center;* Bill Aron: 222 *top;* S. Grandadam: 224; Tony Arruza: 240.
Lu Taskey: 225, 227.
Unicorn/Jeff Greenberg: 82.
Uniphoto: 172 *top.*
Garth Vaughan: 98 *background,* 99 *background.*
Viesti Associates/Joe Viesti: 210 *bottom right.*

Illustrators

David Barnett: 26–27, 30–31, 132, 136, 170–171
Alexander Barsky: 118, 123
Shirley Beckes: 22
Karen Bell: 83
Teresa Berasi: 62
Lisa Blackshear: 228
Alexander Bloch: 258–259
Greta Buchart: 18–19, 20
Kevin Butler: 15, 41, 83, 139, 149, 159, 172–173, 201, 217
Antonio Castro: 16–17
Bobbye Cochran: 124, 130
Dick Cole: 71.
Gwen Connelly: 82, 194–195
Donna Corvi: 86, 87, 88–89
Nerverne Covington: 112, 113, 175
Daniel DelValle: 220–221
Pat DeWitt: 178–179
Barbara Epstein Eagle: 184, 201
Eileen Elterman: 65
Karen Fitz-Maurice: 44
Kristen Goeters: 9, 133, 188–189
Adam Gordon: 174, 257
Susan Greenstein: 54–55
Lane Gregory: 166, 176
Brad Hamann: 94, 114, 126
John Hayson: 76, 106, 140–141, 232–233
Rhonda Hendrichson: 252–253
Steve Henry: 169
Rex Irvine: 138, 204–205
W.B. Johnston: 29
Sommer Keller: 117
Lauren Kiementz-Harte: 14
Dick Kole: 70
Sophia Latto: 224–225
Dora Leder: 52, 104
Al Leiner: 207
Judy Love: 158–159
Diana Magnuson: 42
Steve Marchesi: 28–29
Blaine Martin: 164
Lyn Martin: 202–203
David Scott Meier: 160–161
Deborah Haley Melman: 72–73
Andrew Muonio: 51
Steven Nau: 248
Diane H. Naugle: 90–91, 246
Marty Norman: 186
Kathleen O'Malley: 64, 134–135
Olivia: 25
Debra Page-Trim: 208
Cyndy Patrick: 127
Julie Peterson: 10, 146
Deborah Pinkney: 156
Fernando Rangel: 142–143
Alan Reingold: 10–11, 24, 96
Lainé Roundy: 40, 66–67, 162–163
Margaret Sanfilippo: 32, 68, 103, 116–117
Sally Schaedler: 234
R.J. Shay: 77
Bob Shein: 102
Mark Sparacio: 128–129, 214–215, 230–231, 236
Tom Sperling: 198
Arvis Stewart: 36–37, 180–181
Matt Straub: 48–49
Diane Stubbs: 56–57, 93
Richard Syska: 241
Emily Thompson: 34–35
Gregg Valley: 60, 100–101
Joe Veno: 58–59
Rhonda Voo: 12–13
Dean Wilhite: 97, 152–153
Jenny Williams: 84
Elizabeth Wolf: 80, 81, 212–213
Michael Woo: 45, 107, 111, 144, 154–155, 181, 223, 244–245
Mary O'Keefe Young: 196–197